My Church Was a Mental Hospital

My Church Was a Mental Hospital

BY WARD A. KNIGHTS, JR.

A Pilgrim Press Book *from United Church Press, Philadelphia*

Library of Congress Cataloging in Publication Data

Knights, Ward A   1927-
    My church was a mental hospital.

    "A Pilgrim Press book."
    1. Church work with the mentally ill. 2. Pastoral
psychology. I. Title.
BV4012.3.K58   253.5   74-12018
ISBN 0-8298-0287-8

United Church Press, 1505 Race Street,
Philadelphia, Pennsylvania 19102

To

J.A.C.

and a new lease on life

Contents

Introduction

For quite some time now organizations have been working to make mental illness respectable; I'm not sure they have succeeded. If you're in a group you are aware that rules for polite conversation permit detailed accounts of "when I was in the hospital with my gallbladder." But the same rules forbid talk of mental illness—unless it's somebody else's, and that somebody is fairly distant—and the talk is accompanied by tongue-clucking and sad shakes of the head. Mental hospitals are still places that are shunned. The fact that few states adequately fund their mental hospitals is mute evidence of how too many of us are frightened by this reality in our midst. The fact is that mental illness is scary. It scares people at cocktail parties, and it scares state legislatures too.

Somehow we still think there are two kinds of people: those in mental hospitals (crazy), and everybody else. But as a psychiatrist friend told me, "Institutionalized people are the same as us, only more so."

For nearly fifteen years I was a mental hospital chaplain. It was frustrating, rewarding, confusing, exhilarating, challenging, and it made me grow. I learned about myself, I learned about people, about what's real and what's not. The same as us, indeed!

It's true I was a "mental health professional" but I also knew about those hospitals in a more personal

11

way. I first learned what they were really like when a member of my close family became a statistic—the one out of ten who goes to a mental hospital. Then I learned how these hospitals fail. But I also saw them succeed wonderfully in enhancing life and reintegrating personalities (saving souls).

We've heard far too much about the negative side of our mental hospitals. Snake pit. Looney bin. Booby hatch. Funny farm. You can add to that list, but can you think of a single nickname for a medical hospital? For the sake of those multiple thousands of Americans who spend their lives in the "snake pit," and for the sake of those thousands more who spend at least a portion of their lives there today, we need to understand what they are really like.

So we have this book, *My Church Was a Mental Hospital*. One national organization recently referred to chaplains as a "low-profile" profession. In a day when seminary professors have proclaimed that "God is dead" and when the clergy in general are struggling for credibility and recognition by other professions it is not strange that this may be so. But I'm less concerned about my "profile" than telling the story of the pastoral care of real persons.

In this book Smithville State Hospital (SSH) is not a real hospital, and yet it is. It represents the hospitals at which I have trained and in which I worked. It represents shared experiences with other chaplains engaged in similar work. The people, the situations, are also real in the same sense. Persons, situations, conversations have been presented in such a way that personal and institutional integrity have been preserved.

A word about the chaplain, Arthur King. Any resemblance with the author is more than coincidental. But here also I must admit that Chaplain King seems to have a little more wisdom than I possessed. For one thing, he had the help of "hindsight" which I did not.

I most gratefully acknowledge the help of Mrs. Ethel Gleason, who typed the final manuscript, and of Fr. David McPhee and Fr. James Picchiarini of St. Joseph's Hospital, for their encouragement.

And a special word of appreciation to Kenneth Mitchell and his book *Hospital Chaplain* which inspired me to get to work and share these experiences related to pastoral care in a mental hospital.

1 So What's a Chaplain Anyway?

The Rev. Arthur King had just arrived at Smithville State Hospital. After eight years in the parish ministry and specialized training including two graduate degrees, he felt that here at SSH he was ready to buckle down and make a solid contribution to the healing of persons.

The phone rang. "Yes, this is Chaplain King."

It was Mr. Hoyt who was in charge of the social service program at Smithville. ". . . So anyway I was wondering if you would mind taking Mrs. Baker into town so she could get that new pair of shoes." ". . . Well, Rev. Edwards always helped us out in this sort of thing." ". . . Oh, yeah, well, OK, thanks anyway, Reverend."

He didn't have to say it out loud. Underneath was the question, "What *do* you do, anyway?"

The Rev. E. Thornton Edwards had been Chaplain King's predecessor. He was a retired minister when he came to Smithville State Hospital. Everyone loved him.

He wore a dark suit, was short and thin, was always going around praying with people, and ran errands for the social service department. Of course, he held religious services on Sundays. He smiled at everybody and did not know how to say no. He was the living stereotype of a chaplain. Not an easy man to follow.

The stereotype of the chaplain that often exists is not difficult to understand. The dictionary defines chaplain as an ecclesiastic attached to chapel, military unit, etc., someone who says prayers for meetings. So here we have it, a chaplain is an "ecclesiastic" who is at the hospital to say prayers, and do whatever ecclesiastics do. Obviously this stereotype does not fit the reality of the person and work of those who serve today as chaplains in our hospitals and other institutions. While there may have been a time when such was true of the work done by ecclesiastics (and this is somewhat open to question), it has been less and less true during the last half century as our modern chaplaincy has developed.

Now, let's get ready for a little fun. Taking the lead of Chaplain (Major General) Roy Terry (he gave a really humorous talk to military chaplains on this subject), it might be good for us to consider in a slightly humorous vein the present situation common to many forms of chaplaincy. (After all, usually when we see the humor of a situation we are much closer to the truth.) Chaplain Terry suggests that one myth that must be dispelled is one which sees *the chaplain-as-well-meaning-but-bumbling-ineffectual.*

Here we bring to mind the Beetle Bailey cartoons which show us Chaplain Staneglass. The military somehow more readily lends itself to humor than does a mental hospital. But we can create our own version of

Chaplain Staneglass for the hospital. (After all, TV hospital shows, like MASH, have taken quite a few such liberties.) Our chaplain is so sincere, he wants to do everything for everybody. The chaplain says beautiful prayers for a patient, but the physician has to do the work. The chaplain is doing "depth-counseling" with a patient, but the psychiatrist discharges the patient just as the chaplain is about to enter a crucial phase of therapy. The receptionist says: "The doctor can't see you now chaplain, he's doing something important." (How's your sense of humor doing, Art?) What we are after here, is to see this myth for the humorous thing it is so that we may dispel it (or even "exorcise" it). What we are trying to point out is the way the person and work of chaplain is often stereotyped.

So, let's look at another myth. Here the chaplain is seen as *peddler-of-the-small-picture*. Again, the humor of the situation is not hard to see. The military chaplain gives a lecture on "clean speech" to a group of soldiers who have just returned from a mission where they have killed large numbers of their fellow human beings. (That certainly is ludicrous!) Again, we could create our own cartoon for the hospital. Let's say this cartoon has two pictures. In picture one we see the chaplain, preferably with clerical collar, in the chapel trying to decide which color would be best for the new drapes to be put in the windows. In the other picture profound looking men (obviously professionals) are trying to decide how to get back the hospital's accreditation. (Remember, don't lose your sense of humor, Artie.) All right, we easily see the dictionary definition which carries on this myth, "Chaplain, . . . a person who says the prayers . . .", etc. Here we need considerable demythologizing. This myth also extends directly into the area of the ability of the chaplain to work with patients at the level of their personal and emotional needs. Let's hold a special service of exorcism for this myth! (The psychiatrist E. Mansell Pattison has had a lot to say about the waste of the clergyman's talents and training in our hospitals.)

Another myth is one that many chaplains have special trouble with when it comes to seeing the humor involved (say a special prayer for these chaplains). It is the myth of *chaplain-as-house-priest-or-resident-shaman*. The classic representation of this myth can be found in the book *Patton*. (Or maybe you saw the motion picture.) In this myth the chaplain is a lackey in the house of his overlord. He never questions anything. If the boss says "pray for rain," then he prays for rain. If the boss says "pray for the rain to stop," he prays for the rain to stop. In this myth it is especially important that the chaplain be moderately good-looking (but not overly so), that he always carry about him an air of both dignity and innocence, and that he be present at all formal occasions to add his dignity to the occasion (but, like a child, to be seen more than heard). The Rev. Arthur King had trouble with this myth. He, like some other chaplains, failed to see the humor in all this at times because (1) sometimes he thought maybe this actually was his role, and (2) at times he felt hopelessly trapped in this role and didn't know how to get out of it. Which is all the more reason to see the humor of it all. (But on his better days Art used to say it tickled his fancy a bit to think of himself as a furry rabbit's foot.)

It is obvious, of course, that the myths that apply to the chaplain are also largely applicable to all clergymen, and should be seen in this larger context. Yet the chaplain is not always seen that way. The Rev. Arthur King recalled all too many times when he was greeted by his colleagues in the parish ministry with the humorous question "why did you leave the ministry?" And the following illustrates the point of view of the layman toward chaplains. There was the woman with whom Arthur had done extensive counseling at Smithville State who, in her expression of gratitude for his help, said, at the end of the last session: "You've done so much to help me, I hope that someday you get your own church." (Did he ever have trouble seeing the humor in that one!)

On the Admitting 2 Ward

It was a hot summer day, really hot, and there was no such luxury as air-conditioning at Smithville State Hospital. Being responsible for the pastoral care of twelve hundred people can wear rather heavily if it is taken seriously. You are buoyed up by a breakthrough here and there.

The call finally comes. It is the secretary from the clinical director's office. "Chaplain King, Dr. Cohen says he would be pleased to have you attend the diagnostic meeting. It will begin on Ward 1A in about ten minutes in the conference room just inside the door."

Dr. I. Cohen was one of the greatest assets that SSH had. You never thought of calling him by his first name. "Reverend King," he said to me as I sat in front of his desk, "I must admit that I don't know why we didn't think to invite you to the staff meeting on the admitting ward."

He didn't have to say why, I knew. It doesn't take long to find staff members who are willing to share what's really going on. The Rev. E. Thornton Edwards had attended a couple of meetings. He got involved over his head. Said a lot of things that didn't make sense. It was so embarrassing to everyone that they just forgot to notify him when the next meeting was held. Maybe Dr. Cohen had repressed the memory of those embarrassing experiences so thoroughly that he really didn't know why he had not thought to invite the new chaplain to the staff meeting.

Keys, keys, you even need a key to get into the bathroom. But it does give you a feeling of power. At least *you* have keys. Then there is the old joke about that being the best way to tell staff from patients. A lot of truth in that.

The patient being diagnosed was a Mr. Miller. First there was a fairly thorough presentation by a social worker, Mr. Aiken. He presented a detailed and rather long history. Then the psychologist followed with a summary report of several tests, particularly the Rorschach. (He loved that test.) After that the ward physician gave a detailed report on the patient's physical condition. Finally the nurse reported on the patient's behavior. Everything was precise, impersonal, somewhat like a top-level executive meeting of a large corporation. Now everyone turned to the chairman of the board. One hour and fifteen minutes had been spent in preparation. Dr. I. Cohen said almost nothing during that time.

"Manic-Depressive, suicidal tendencies, a series of ECT as soon as possible." The meeting was over.

ECT (electro-convulsive therapy) has been said by some to be almost a miracle cure for many forms of mental illness. It has also been called—even by psychiatrists—an inhuman means of modern torture. At Smithville State Hospital it was used liberally.

I had to deal with the patient's wife. I held Mrs. Miller's hand firmly while she cried. She had signed the consent paper so that the ECT could be used on her husband.

"What else could I do?" she said. "But don't a certain number of people die or receive fractures?"

"Yes." (Don't give false comfort here, try to stay with her, don't let it get to you too, or you won't be of any help.)

She seemed to gasp almost violently, "When I saw him hanging there I thought he was dead . . ." Then she cried for about ten minutes, it seemed like an hour.

Smithville did not medicate patients prior to "shock." (In some hospitals when ECT is used, medication is given which relaxes the patient and eases the psychological and physical shock.) Convulsions were usually quite violent.

Mrs. Miller asked me to be present during the ECT. "Vell, I don't know iff ve could haf you there ven da treatment iss given, after all iss medical procedure."

I somehow always had the feeling that I wasn't really sure whether or not any communication was taking place when I was talking to Dr. Zekens. No doubt he was a brilliant man, but I always thought he should have taken a course in the use of the English language. He had responsibility for all ECT at Smithville State Hospital.

This has to be handled carefully. Is this a time for a lecture to the good doktor on the relationship of religion to medicine? ("After all, doctor, we did use to be in the same business, at least at one time in history.")

But Dr. Zekens surprises you. "I vill call Dictor

Coven and ask. . . . Yess, iss alright, but please you sit down on chair in corner, don't want you to fall on floor." So Dr. Cohen came through again.

Mrs. Miller had practically begged me to be present during that first shock treatment. She wanted to be there, but that was not allowed. "Why can't I be there?" she said. "He's my husband, and if he might die or be hurt why don't I have a right to be there?"

"It is hard to take." (Wasn't I playing this one cool. I had to resist the inclination to say: "Get a lawyer, demand your right to be with him.")

I was going through a corridor in "C" building when one of the psychiatric aides called, "Hey, Rev., did they find you?"

"No." Mr. Miller wanted to see me.

It was strange, but Mr. Miller had never spoken a word to me before. Each time I had visited him he looked at the floor or out the window and didn't seem to even acknowledge my presence—or hardly anyone else's for that matter. But now he had actually asked to see me. It had been nearly a week since he had finished his series of shock treatment.

It was hard to realize that this was the same man. He talked on and on. Not all of it made sense, at least not to me. He even looked different, relaxed, fewer wrinkles. Would I please tell his wife he wanted to see her right away, he missed her very much. To me it did seem somewhat of a miracle—sort of like the dead being raised.

More patients on the admission wards. Sometimes as many as ten new ones a week. You could spend all your time there, with the patients, their families, the staff, in the staff meetings. But there are eleven hundred and fifty others waiting.

Miss Primm stopped me as I came into the admitting ward to see Mr. Miller. She had just been admitted.

"You're a Reverend, aren't you?"

"Yes, I'm Chaplain King."

"Then you have to help me to get out of here. This place is run by the anti-Christ. I was in the process of preparing to be a missionary. And then it happened—the devil started coming to me—he lured me into this place. You've got to get me out of here so I can do the Lord's work as I'd planned."

Everyone has trouble dealing with a patient who talks like this. They are pretty aggressive. Their religious language tends to stop you short for a while. Naturally you don't want to help the devil in his work; of course you want people to do the Lord's work. You envy those staff members without any interest in religion, they can just shrug it all off. Miss Primm's case was used in a nursing seminar as one of classic religious delusions.

"You aren't going to help me then?"

"Yes, I will help you, but I can't get you out of here right now."

"Then you are of the anti-Christ too, you are of your father the devil, and you like the rest will burn in the lake that burns for ever and ever." She literally stomped away from me. Maybe later she would remember I accepted all this and maintained my offer to help her.

Mr. Miller and I had met a number of times now. The euphoria was really gone today.

"I feel so ashamed. How can I ever face going home after what I did. Everyone knows." It's hard to take a sixty-eight-year-old man's crying.

"It won't be easy." (Careful, give him support, but

don't minimize the problems that will be ahead for him.)

"It'll be just like it was before, and I can't take that anymore." (Loud gasp like he was trying to gulp in air.)

(Silence) ". . . you can't take what . . . ?"

(Long sigh) "I just didn't want to live any more. I just didn't want to live. Now, right now, I can feel the same feeling coming back. I know I'll do the same thing again, I know it, I know it." (Silence, he stares at the floor.)

Well, Arthur King, what do you say now? You know that any statement like: "All things are possible to those who believe," or "What you need is more faith," are totally irrelevant. About all you can do is to be with him, to let him know you feel that feeling with him, and then somehow offer hope. Now you begin to see the meaning of hope, its importance in life.

". . . and give us hope where there is no hope . . . Amen."

Miss Primm grabs you as you are fumbling with your keys; she is really aggressive. You should have gone home an hour ago. It takes fifteen minutes before you can get away. Then dear old motherly Gwen Smith, R.N. stops you at the door. She looks very solicitous and motherly.

"I hope you don't think I'm trying to tell you what to do, Reverend, but after you talked to Mr. Miller today he cried for a long time. Maybe you shouldn't see him anymore for a while."

It has been a long day, and there would be another like it tomorrow.

I had the fantasy that I had been dismissed for the day by Patton.

The
Prison
3 Ward

It's one thing to be invited to a staff meeting, but it's another thing to be really part of a team. You've got to earn that, and in your seminary training, even your clinical training, they don't tell you how. You remain open, work your head off, pray, wait for a little luck.

I visited in the prison ward infrequently. It wasn't that I didn't want to be there more. It was partly the hassle—they were very sparing about the keys, said it was "maximum security." Of course it was a hospital ward, not a prison ward, but everyone knew it was really a prison, a place for "psychos" to be sent for evaluation or "prolonged care."

Every morning about ten o'clock I usually stopped by the coffee shop because I was pretty sure to find a cross section of staff there. Those informal contacts were pretty important. Over coffee, and out from behind desks, you got to know each other as human beings.

I hadn't met him yet, but I knew who it was. "We have todomoreforthepatients on maximum ward." It was Manuel Garcia, M.D. who had just come to us for a year residency in psychiatry. He was young, full of ideas, wouldn't take no for an answer on anything he wanted to do bad enough, and had a way of talking so fast that he ran all his words together.

I sat down quietly with my cup of coffee.

"It is criminal onourpart tosoneglect these persons." It took a while to get used to his speech. It almost seemed like he was singing.

"There just isn't any time."

"We all have case loads about twice as large as we should have."

"It's a question of where to concentrate the effort. That group is probably the most difficult here."

"Why don't we try a little psychodrama over there?" The Rev. Arthur King finally spoke up.

Man Garcia spun around like he had been shot. He was practically vibrating. "That would be wild, really wild. Don't think we'vemetyet."

"I'm Arthur King."

"He's the *Reverend* Arthur King, our *chaplain*."

Man did another interesting thing; he seemed to deflate. "The Rev. . . ." The silence was rather conspicuous.

"It would never work. Too dangerous. You'd have the whole place torn down in a week. You can't encourage expression of feelings and ideas over there. It would never work at all." Our psychologist, Herbert Davenport, had disagreed with me again. He had given his professional opinion. He always seemed to exude satisfaction in putting Arthur King and his ideas in their place.

Man didn't say anything, he seemed to be thinking. Somehow the conversation seemed to be over, the coffee break had been too long, everyone hurried back to their offices, or whatever.

As sort of a parting shot Man said, "Look me up in my office when youhavetime *Reverend*, wecantalk moreabout whatyoucall prison ward."

Man Garcia was really a delightful guy. By comparison with the rest of the staff he thought "wild" thoughts. But he had to admit he had never seen a *chaplain* before.

"I get the feeling at times that some of our staff don't really want to try anything new." (Have to be careful now Art, some of your anger is coming out. Well, maybe it says this guy is somehow different.)

"Wish Iknewmore about psychodrama. But know-enough to think maybe might work. We did quiteabit psychodrama at my hospital. What you know about it?"

"Well, Man (it was easy to call him that, it just fit somehow), I just happen to be a certified alter ego."

We had a winning combination and we knew it.

Dr. Cohen gave his permission, with sort of a twinkle in his eye. I think he was beginning to like me. You could see that he thought Man and I were a strange combination to be doing therapy with a group of psychopaths. It didn't take much perception to see that he was quite pleased.

At the first session the bare meeting room seemed like an armed camp. Four of the huskiest aides were there, two nurses, including the nursing supervisor (I'd already come to realize that *he* was the real power in that building). We had decided to go for broke. All nineteen patients from one wing filed in.

You could sense the pent-up feelings. Hostility seemed to be throbbing in the group. But we got through the first session. Actually we did more than that. We reenacted scenes of breaking and entering. Patients took the roles of arresting officers. At one point

I took the role of "the psychiatrist." I stroked my imaginary chin whiskers and said: "Vell your problem is that you have nev-ver been appropriately socialized, vat you need is treatment, but more than I can give, must zend you to hospital." (Careful, Art, you may get a fist in the mouth.) They descended on me, shouted at me. "We need help and you send us to this stinkin' place."

In Man's apartment that evening after supper we relived the entire group session. It had been good! Contrary to the expectations of some of our fellow staff members there had been no riot, and it was the *patients* who asked for more. We toasted our new working relationship.

It surprises you at first, you think that in a place like a mental hospital you will be working with a group of people who have worked through all their hang ups. You think they must all be familiar with the latest therapeutic approaches. But you find that even the staff is human. After a while, when you have digested that, you're ready to become part of the team. You finally realize that the concept of the "team" is only a concept. You work with people, "professional" people, but still people. You can't take them for granted. You can't let them take you for granted. You find, when you're honest, that you tend to stereotype them, just as they stereotype you.

But you're going to break the stereotype of the chaplain.

"Chaplain King, 310 . . . Chaplain King, 310." It was the squawk box. One of the things that made people seem important at SSH was the number of times you heard their names. It wasn't like a general hospital, where you seemed to hear doctors' names over the speakers all day long. Pages here were infrequent.

So now you're beginning to feel important—careful, *Chaplain*.

There was getting to be some spin-off from the psychodrama sessions on the prison ward.

"Reverend King, I would like to see you about a patient. If you have the time could you come to my office now?"

Carol Winfield, M.D. was one of the few board certified psychiatrists at SSH. I don't think she had ever said more than "Hello" to me before. The staff generally thought of her as stuck-up, aloof, untouchable. But nobody, nobody, ever doubted for one moment her competence or her dedication to her patients. Everyone wondered why someone with her qualifications stayed at Smithville.

Dr. Winfield had her own coffeepot. You never saw her in the coffee shop. She poured two cups of coffee. Her office was more like a living room. From the window beside her desk there was a beautiful view out across the hospital farm and the countryside beyond.

"Chaplain, I think you can help me."

"I would consider it a pleasure, Dr. Winfield."

"Dr. Garcia has asked that one of the patients from the prison ward be transferred to one of my floors."

By the time she stopped, Dr. Winfield had talked for over thirty minutes, giving the history of the patient and her plan for therapy. You had the feeling that she really did care. Was this the "aloof, the untouchable" doctor? How much too ready we all are to judge others!

"Dr. Cohen feels that we need to provide a better link between the prison ward and the treatment wards."

"I will be doing therapy with John (the patient) which will be confrontive and demanding. It will not be easy for him. I will see him twice a week. When he is ready he will be given a regular job to occupy his time. I want you to be a *father* to him.

"For obvious reasons I can't do that for him." Her smile was mischievous—and very human.

Sociopaths are difficult people to work with. One of their problems seems to be that they just don't learn from their experience. Some authorities think they just have to grow old and "burn out" before they really change. There were times when we felt that might be true of John.

After two months of careful work in therapy, a great deal of "fathering," increased work responsibility within the building, first on the ward and then on the central kitchen of the building, John was granted his often-repeated request to be allowed to work on the grounds-crew which mowed lawns, tended flowers, and other such tasks. Of course it meant more freedom. We felt certain he could handle it.

The decision to allow John the freedom of the grounds was not easy to make. There was more than the strictly "therapeutic" aspect to the decision. Since John had been sent to the hospital by the court this meant the hospital had legal responsibility for him. The hospital has to be rather careful to avoid "bad press" whenever possible. All the goodwill the staff tried to build up in the community over a long period of time could be wiped out by one headline in the local paper screaming: "Dangerous Mental Patient on Loose from Smithville State Hospital."

In some cases these headlines made you laugh because they were so inappropriate to the patient involved. This really was not the case with John. His

offenses had been very serious and he had been la-
belled "a menace to society."

John had "eloped" his first day on the grounds-crew.
First he was there and then he wasn't. Nobody knew
quite how it happened. But Dr. Winfield and I were
optimistic. Our greatest misgiving was that the matter
had to be reported to the state police. That usually did
nothing except create a lot of bad publicity. In a hurried staff meeting it was decided that John was testing
the "limits," and also testing the genuineness of our
concern for him. It was felt that the best thing we
could do was to organize a "posse," cover the immedi-
ate area, and find him as soon as possible.

Most of the psychiatric aides were quite familiar
with the area around the hospital. It was just about
dusk when he was spotted running across a field. We
were glad we found him before the state police.

John was back on the prison ward when his "father"
saw him the next morning.

You didn't get discouraged by this sort of thing because you knew it was all part of the therapy. *You* were
being tested now. Can you give him the father's love
he never had? Can you love him?

While you're on the prison ward you stop to see a
newly admitted patient.

"Hello, I'm Chaplain King."

"Whatsa a chaplain?"

"I'm a clergyman, a minister."

"Get the hell outa here. You're probably like all a'
the rest o' them comin' here to save my soul and tell me
how sinful I am, and fill me full of a lot of junk."

You excuse yourself and leave, your love seems to
have about run out for today. But—maybe tomorrow—
there's always tomorrow.

4 Bummin' Around

Sometimes when you get involved in too many things and you feel like you've just got to get away, you do what Arthur King calls "bummin' around."

You just walk down the corridors, look around, you go down to the power house, you go to the green house, you go to the farm. Mental hospitals really made quite a mistake when they did away with the farm. The administration says that it is "no longer economically feasible," but it certainly is therapeutic.

"Hello, I'm Arthur King. I'm chaplain here, I think I saw you the other day but don't think we really had a chance to get acquainted."

"Yes, I'm Don Hanson, in charge of the farm."

"Well, Don, I just stopped around to see what is going on. Could you, if you have the time, show me around a little bit?"

"Sure, be glad to. I was just going out to the apple orchard, so come on along."

Don was just made for the job, he enjoyed the outdoors, and he seemed to have an intuitive understanding of patients.

33

"Now down here this morning I have twenty patients pickin' apples, look at those people work—there they are, down that row of trees right there. You know, we have one of the best apple crops in this area. Supply the dining room with apples for the whole year 'round." You could see the pride in his face. The apples were good too; it didn't take much urging to sample one.

Don was saying, "See that fellow over there, hey now that's really a remarkable one. Practically catatonic when they sent him down here to the farm. But do you know, in less than a week's time that fellow really came alive—one of our best pickers now. You wouldn't believe it. You know I really think that's what's wrong with a lot of people today—too far away from the soil, aren't really in touch with life—really makes me feel good."

You know what he means Arthur King, right about now you'd like to get up on a ladder and start picking a few apples yourself. Brings back memories of your boyhood doesn't it? Out there in the quiet of the apple orchard you feel that you're really alive, somehow a part of things. You really have to hold yourself back to not accept the offer and become part of that crew and pick some of those apples. Sometimes your work seems to deal with so many intangibles that you'd welcome the chance to get hold of something solid, something you could really get your teeth into!

But you just came to take a look, to see what was goin' on.

Smithville State Hospital may have been criticized for a lot of things, but it couldn't be criticized for its farm. Not only did it have one of the best apple orchards around, but it had a prize herd of cows, good barns, and a piggery that was really second to none.

The farm surrounded the grounds. There were those who wondered why SSH was built "out in the middle of nowhere," but Don knew why.

The farm sort of surrounded SSH. As you went around the edge of the grounds you saw the vegetable gardens, the acres of corn, the flower beds. Those people working in the flower beds really looked contented. Sure didn't look very "crazy" to you, did they Art?

"Hope you don't mind, Reverend, but I have to swing by one of the fields and drop off a part for one of the tractors."

It was all over too soon.

"Can I drop you some place, *Reverend?*"

You couldn't take that anymore.

"Please call me Art."

"O.K., Art, but, uh, I feel a little funny callin' a Reverend by his first name, but yeah, O.K. *Art.*"

"Yeah, drop me off at the powerhouse, Don, if that's on your way, I've been wanting to take a look at that operation."

The noise, the whine of the generators, is pretty bad. SSH generated all its own electricity. In fact when you looked at it SSH was almost a self-sufficient community.

Next to the powerhouse was the laundry. A lot of patients worked there, got paid for it too, five dollars a month! The papers always screamed about that—"slave labor" they called it. Most of the patients there were glad to have a job, something to do, a little pocket money. All their other needs—food, a room, clothing, medical care—were taken care of. Not the best, but on the whole probably better than most of their friends back home.

One of the things that struck you about these "outlying parts" of the hospital was the fact that they seemed so totally different from the wards, the rooms, the corridors inside.

Yet somehow the hospital had been fortunate in collecting a staff that was convinced it was doing something to help people. I knew that the people here were getting wages much less than they could make in similar jobs outside. But most of them were motivated by some pretty personal things.

George, in the hospital garage, told me, "I quit here a coupla times, but I always come back. Somehow it's different here, ya know you're part of somethin', ya help people. Ah, I guess I don't do as much as you chaplain or some of the doctors, but I kinda feel I'm part of it, ya know? My mother 'fore she died—she was a patient here—and that's O.K., God rest her soul . . . But you know I really do feel like I'm doin' somethin', ya know what I mean?"

Yes, Art, you know what he meant.

You almost hate to go back into that building again, and you know you ought to be in your office, or visiting new patients, or . . . , but you stop off at the photolab. You know that when you get sick of listening to people's problems sometimes you can always go and chat with Frank. Frank's job is to take pictures of patients when they come in and to do a lot of other things around the hospital, but the photolab is his "office."

Frank is pure "country."

He worked his way up to this job the hard way.

"Yep, I used to work on the road crew. Wasn't really too bad, but I had a chance to get this job. Hey, *Chappie*, we're really glad you're around here, ya know. Glad you stop around and talk once in a while. Does get a little lonesome here. Hey, some time ya got nothin' else to do stop by my place, I got some prize white Leghorns like you ain't never seen."

"O.K., Frank, but only if ya cook one of them for me."

But now Arthur King you're feeling a little bit guilty, you always do when you "bum around," and so you hurry back to your office.

You really hate that office, because on that desk you know is a pile of letters, memos, files and who knows what, that seems to get higher every day.

You did a little calculating once, and you figured that if you wrote a letter to everybody you should, ex-patients, relatives, former staff members, clergy interested in training, etc., you would be writing letters at least four hours every day.

Sometimes even you, Arthur King, get a little angry that the administration seemed to forget that even chaplains need secretarial help—someone to type letters, put notes in patient records, write up notes of meetings, file patient census cards, run errands, answer the phone—but you do the best you can.

"Persons first, paper work second," nice motto, but oh so difficult to follow.

You look at the pile of letters on your desk. On top are six letters that came this morning from relatives of patients. You'd better answer those. Probably some of them are going to stop by your office and want to know how things are going for their relatives who are in your hospital. You'd better have some answers. That means you've got to see more patients, try to track down some psychiatrists, then sit down at the typewriter—that monster over in the corner—that will be your penance for "bummin' around."

Clinical Pastoral 5 Education

Students have a way of treading where angels fear to walk. They tend to sharpen up issues, they send you scurrying for better answers.

Smithville State Hospital had never had clergy there for training before. One of the reasons the Reverend Arthur King was there was to initiate a program of Clinical Pastoral Education (CPE).

CPE has brought about a quiet (well, mostly) revolution in theological education. Under the impetus of men like Anton T. Boisen, Richard C. Cabot, Russell L. Dicks, clergymen began to come out of their ivory towers and learn from "the living human documents."

Where better to learn about the real "stuff" of life than in hospitals, prisons, mental health clinics, schools for the mentally retarded. You want to carry the message of salvation? Then go where the lost are! (You see the preacher in Art come out every once in a while.)

Putting together a CPE program isn't easy. First you have to establish your place on the "team." You have to break down the stereotypes of the clergy. The hospital has to have an honest appreciation of the chaplain. When you think this has happened you begin to plan for training programs. It's an administrative nightmare. Meanwhile you have to carry on your regular ministry. You have to attend meetings, follow procedures, standards, guidelines. Somehow you make it.

A program to learn how to be a chaplain.

A program in which you learn how to be a pastoral counselor.

A program in which you get psychoanalyzed.

A way of learning pastoral care.

An experience in which theology is forgotten.

What is clinical pastoral education?

CPE is difficult to define. We say that it has the objective of providing for the learning of pastoral practice in a clinical setting, a setting which allows for the integration of knowledge from medicine, psychology, psychiatry, and other behavioral sciences—all in relation to pastoral care.

The key word, of course, is clinical, it is a "bedside" learning experience. It means that the student, be he seminarian, clergyman, or other, learns pastoral care in relationship to people, and he learns this primarily through concrete individual experiences with persons.

CPE in the beginning, and still largely today, was patterned after the medical model. Just as the physician and surgeon do not come to full competence by merely reading books in medical school, neither can the clergyman be truly competent without practical experience in ministry to people without intensive clinical training. As with persons in the field of medicine, so in pastoral care, the student functions under close supervision, and his work is subject to critical analysis.

We say that this process enables the student to learn about himself, his pastoral role, the persons to whom he ministers, and the context of his ministry.

Beyond this we also say that the basic CPE experience affords the student an opportunity, under pastoral supervision, along with his fellow students, to explore and evaluate (1) his function as a clergyman, (2) his personal and pastoral identity, (3) his relationship to other professional disciplines, and ability to think theologically about his experience, (4) his ability to communicate his faith meaningfully, (5) his interpersonal relationships, and the processes by which he grows, and (6) his attitudes, values, and assumptions about life.

The content of the individual program is usually composed of eight factors. (1) They are full-time training programs, given basically in terms of 400-hour quarters of ten weeks. (2) Involvement consists of responsible ministry to persons in varying conditions of need. (3) Participation is in a peer group of no fewer than three persons with opportunity for small group interaction. (4) Ministry is exercised in the context of staff relationships. (5) Individual and group supervision is performed by an ACPE certified supervisor. (6) Regular reporting and evaluating of specific instances of ministry is done. (7) The student is enlisted as a partner in the learning process by helping him identify his goals, planning for his learning and evaluating his progress. (8) Theory is brought to bear on the practical work of ministry. This includes the theoretical understanding of the person, his relationships, and the context in which he ministers. Essentially this involves assisting the student to clarify his operational concepts and styles of ministry. Structures useful for this purpose are seminars, group experiences, lectures, etc.

How easy it is to set forth these things on paper. How much more difficult to actualize them!

Each student who comes for training is a unique individual. He has his own motivation, his own goals, his own personal "style."

Adam Frank said, "Actually, the reason I'm here, since you want us to be really honest about it, is because my seminary requires it. What I really wanted to do this summer was to spend the whole vacation with my friends in the Bahamas." You wonder if you did the right thing by accepting him.

George Jones was a parish minister; he had been in the ministry for nineteen years. George said, "It just seems like nobody pays any attention to you unless you have all sorts of credentials, so I decided to get some." But that wasn't the only motivation that George had. George was failing in his pastoral ministry, his church had given him the summer off in the hope that he would get more training and be able to return to them and be of effective service. If he didn't make the grade he didn't know what he would do. (What does a clergy-man *do* when he is forced to leave the ministry? What's he good for?)

Carlton Smith was a seminary senior. He had a strong undergraduate background in psychology. His father was a clergyman. He said, "I'm here because I want to learn more about the deeper motivations of people. I want to find out if all I've learned about personality theory is really true or not, and I want to find out what it really means to be a pastor to people." With that one, how could we miss?

Mary Reynolds was a senior seminary student who had chosen the institutional chaplaincy as her field of specialization in the pastoral ministry. "I want to be a chaplain, and I've got to beat this thing about women not being as good as men in the ministry." We certainly had our job cut out for us on this one.

Father Bee was a priest who had served about five years in a parish as an assistant. He said, "I've been hearing a lot lately about 'clinical training' and I've been wrestling with the problem of how the sacramental ministry can be made more relevant to the needs of my people. I hope I can find that out here."

At the beginning of the program the students spent two weeks on the wards working as psychiatric aides. They did this anonymously. It's a strange thing, but people often tend to act differently when the clergy is around. Usual behavior is often abandoned, and people start talking about religion and stop swearing. Not always, though. Sometimes they will swear and use four-letter words (*not* love, hope, etc.) just to get a "rise" out of the clergy.

Just being on the wards, observing, evaluating, thinking, helping—it does something. The hospital begins to change from being a snake pit—an infinitely complicated nightmare of patients, staff, procedures, rules, locks, bars—it slowly begins to come into focus, you begin to feel part of it. It scares the hell out of you at first, but you struggle with it, you reach out to people, you talk about your fears, about your Uncle Joe who died in a mental hospital, about how you've thought at times maybe you were crazy too. You let it all hang out.

Once that experience is under your belt you become

a chaplain, well a "student" chaplain anyway. You feel a new sense of being part of the team.

Maybe the use of the term chaplain could be improved upon. Perhaps there ought to be another word used when referring to a clergyman who serves in a hospital.

The Rev. George W. Jones, B.A., B.D. came practically charging into my office. To say he looked "visibly shaken" was an understatement.

"You said we were *chaplains* here for the summer." (Said it *very* threateningly.)

"Yes, that's right."

"Well, being a *chaplain* is worse than being a *pastor*." He's staring blankly out the window. "I don't think I know what I am anymore. (There was a long pause during which he seemed to compose himself, then turned almost fiercely on me.) Being a chaplain is *shit*."

You know there is a lot more to it than what title a person goes by. George has got a lot of work to do this summer. He's got a lot to learn about himself. But you can't help but have reservations about the word chaplain.

Chaplain Tom Harris wrote a very interesting paper in which he strongly objects to the very use of the term chaplain. Let's try to keep our sense of humor and take a look at what he says. He says he has had the occasion far too often, as I have, of seeing chaplain spelled *chaplin*. Do we have a Freudian slip here? Is today's chaplain really more like the *comic* figure of Charlie Chaplin than the compassionate figure of Saint Martin who shared his "capella" with a beggar? Perhaps to many he is, and also, perhaps he is in large part to blame. Sometimes in his humility he has failed in aggressiveness, and his efforts to be profound in service have been all too plainly seen in their incongruous reality as a poor caricature of good old "Charlie." I don't blame Tom. At times I also find the term chaplain a very uncomfortable one.

In his paper Tom also used the descriptive word jerk in relation to the chaplain. Through this he made reference to those chaplains who are like puppets. When the "man up above" pulls strings, they jump. Here Tom wasn't thinking of the heavenly-man-up-above model, but rather the chaplain as "property-of-the-prince." In this model the chaplain sees his main job as upholding the status quo. Tom talked about the chaplain as one who blesses the nobles and preserves his warm place by the fire—a castrated flunky of the court. I guess that must have been somewhat the way George felt when he came into the office.

Tom even got a little more specific. He talked about the chaplain supporting the myths of the medical profession, especially the myth of the physician as magician and flawless healer. And then there is the chaplain who spends most of his time encouraging, and listening to, all the hostility that should rightly be directed toward the psychiatrist!

Well, Tom certainly gives us something to think about, doesn't he? Is that what a chaplain is, an upholder of the status quo? May he be pitied if that is what he is, for he is indeed then a tragicomical caricature of a man, a puppet on a string rather than a man of freedom and responsibility.

It was issues like this that were discussed in individual and group sessions. Usually every afternoon, after the students had completed their pastoral contacts, we met for an hour and a half in a seminar session. Mornings were usually divided between didactic and clinical experiences. Psychiatrists helped us to understand psychiatry and the way it seeks to bring about mental healing. Social service shares from its skill in working with the broad social dimensions of the lives of people. Psychology imparts insights in how we can understand personality, how we can go about the process of counseling. Patients taught us about human nature, about what it means to hear and see a thing that isn't there (except that it *is* there inside them), about how difficult it is to face up responsibly to life, about how even religion can be used to distort life and rob it of its meaning.

You continue to struggle with your professional identity. Tom brings us to another dimension of the chaplain's identity, that of *prophet*. (Don't let that word frighten you away.) You often see the chaplain trying to handle his anxiety over the realization that he is a puppet by turning to the role of prophet, and an angry one at that. He conjures up fantasies of an age-old prophet standing someplace on a high hill throwing invectives at a heathen city. Who should better be able to denounce the system? After all, doesn't he speak for God? Clergymen are especially susceptible to the idea that their words are God's will. So, when tension breaks out, and the chapl(a)in (I hope you didn't miss that) feels slighted and ignored Tom says that under what he calls guidance from heaven he becomes as uncooperative as hell.

Now, you understand we are talking here of being a prophet in something other than the biblical sense, we are talking of it as a defensive reaction used by the chapl(a)in who is not ready to face his situation through mature, creative encounter and dialogue. In the same way the chaplain can retreat into his role as priest. He can simply perform his "sacred services" and do little else. There is always a special risk because often other professionals think this is all he ought to do anyway.

Well, Tom thinks that the chaplain would find a better identity as a *jester*. (You just can't miss the humor in all this.) But think of the jester in court. He is dressed in attire different from all the others, he has on a peculiar cap with bells on it (and a strange collar around his neck?). He is preferably short, ugly, and perhaps uncoordinated. (I'll bet you're laughing right now.) But the jester can do something that no one else in the court would dare to do, he can stand up to the baron. He is the only one who seems to be able to do the humanizing thing. He sticks pins into pretentious people. With a tone-deaf voice he sings a would-be song which, in its hilarious way, points to the foolishness of some decision of the baron. Under the guise of a liltingly funny poem he points up to the baron how little he understands the real needs of his subjects.

But the jester's role isn't easy and sometimes, as Tom says, more than one banquet hall has heard the sound of a rolling jester's head (minus body) with bells and all, as it rolled into a corner.

Well, *Chaplain* King, you certainly are learning a lot from your students.

6 Extended Care

Sometimes people who work around mental hospitals for some time are accused of getting "callous," of getting so used to living with tragedy of all kind that the sense of perspective is lost.

As you are working on the admission wards, working with students, you tend to almost forget that there are many patients who are at the hospital for what has been called "extended care." That such care is extended there is no doubt, but sometimes you wonder if there is enough true care in the intended sense of therapy, of trying to return the person to society.

In some hospitals, the past decade has seen a remarkable reduction of patients in this category. In many cases it has come about because true treatment plans were made and carried out. In other situations it seems to have come about at the expense of any care for persons who are now left to degenerate and die on the skid rows of our cities or in the squalid shacks of the back country.

Your students don't let you forget this either.

"My God, Chaplain, I could hardly believe it!" Adam Frank had just come back from his first day on one of our "extended care" wards—more appropriately known as "back wards."

"Something bothering you, Adam?"

"It's like . . . like . . . yeah, *hell*, that's what it's like. How could ya describe it any other way. I could have been down on the beautiful beaches in the Bahamas. . . . Instead, where am I?"

"Right here, I hope. Something happen?"

"Something happen? What kind of a thing to say is that?"

I could see Adam was pretty angry about something. When students don't let anger out in appropriate places you know that a lot of it will probably come your way.

"What happened?"

"I'll tell you what happened. There was feces on the floor over there, I almost stepped in it. Oh God, what an experience." He melted down into the chair.

Adam was a member of a very high church denomination. He-always was dressed immaculately. You could almost have predicted his reaction.

"Jeees, Chaplain, it was awful, they actually slobbered on me. They aren't human beings at all. They smell so bad I wanted to chuck-up. And nobody seems to give a damn. The aides were in the office playing cards."

"It's really hard to take, isn't it?" Somehow that reply almost seemed callous—here is a student really hurting inside, and all you can say is "It's really hard to take, isn't it?" But what else can you say? How can you tell him how it tears you apart too? You want to give him some of the answers you've found, but you know he has to find them for himself.

"Hard to take? Jeees, don't use that nondirective stuff on me. I'm not a patient, but if I go over there any more maybe I will be. Take me off that ward. I won't go back, it's hopeless, yeah, hope, hope, there's no hope."

"There's no pastoral ministry that has any relevance there, is that it?"

"That's right, not for me anyway. What could anyone do there?"

"How about trying to answer your own question?"

"How can I answer it, they never talked about things like this at the 'Sem' in any course I took. It even makes you wonder what kind of a God . . ."

Adam was beginning to grapple with the hard reality of the back wards at Smithville State Hospital. Far too many people had come to SSH, observed what Adam had observed and then went back home demanding the resignation of the hospital superintendent, or even a grand jury investigation. It's a lot easier to criticize, to point out what's wrong, than to do something about it.

One of the realities on the back wards was the chronic lack of staff.

It is 10:00 P.M. and you are walking through the corridors of "B" building. You're not usually there at that time, but occasionally you are around at odd hours, to meet staff members on shifts other than the day shift, to see what goes on at these other times.

"Who's that? Oh, hi, Chaplain. If you've been doing any praying lately would you please pray for the staff here." Pat Bruno is one of the "burly" aides that worked the 3-11 shift.

"Didn't know you were such a religious man, Pat."

"All kidding aside, Chaplain, the staff here is going to go bananas themselves one of these nights. Look at me here, a guy didn't show up on number 2 ward so I've got to cover both wards 1 and 2. Sixty-three patients on my ward, fifty-nine on his. I can't be in two places at once!"

It's a familiar story to you. A matter of chronic shortage of staff. Ridiculously low salaries to begin with, and no money to hire more. Even staff members get sick occasionally and don't show up for work.

The hospital is really caught in a vicious circle. Because the salaries were so low there were twenty vacant positions for psychiatric aides when the state legislature met last year. One legislator, who had long championed economy in state government, gave a long eloquent speech on economy. Eliminating the vacant positions at the hospital would be one way of saving money—after all if the hospital was running without these positions being filled then obviously the hospital didn't need the *extra* help. When you're caught in this kind of bind it's really hard to do anything.

Why was there not more "treatment" on these wards? Basically what it came down to was that there just wasn't any staff to do the treatment.

"Man" Garcia stopped by my office, something he rarely did. He was looking beat. His year's time at Smithville State was nearly up.

"BelievemeArt, I really happy tobethinking about leaving. No one candowhat they expect youtodo here. We do good things on prison ward, but all the other patients, I responsible for one-hundred-fifty now. What canIdo?" I'd never heard Man talk this way before.

"I know."

"The system doesn't work. Patients just pluguphere. Have no placetogo. Even when they arewell enough nobody takethem home. Who works thatoutnow? Nobody, not any social workers tospeakof, no money." He really was down today. Little wonder, I happened to know that while he was only required to work a forty-hour week he rather routinely worked closer to sixty hours.

"Yes, Iwilbe glad to go."

"You're lucky. Think of me, I'll still be here." (That kind of stuff often tends to be catching. When you let it out you have to be careful or you infect a lot of other people.)

"I'm sorry, Art, sorry, I didn't mean to dump it all on you."

"It's O.K., Man, having you here has really been great for all of us."

Understanding the reality of the situation doesn't do anything for the patient. It makes you go home from work at night feeling you did what little you could do. But you never can escape feeling a little guilty that you didn't do enough. At times you feel like you should maybe run for public office and bring some pressure to bear politically, or you feel like writing angry letters to the newspaper editor, or to the governor. And sometimes you do!

2 Ward was typical of the back wards at SSH. It was a locked ward. It housed about sixty patients in a space that was designed—a hundred years ago—to house forty patients. The room at the end of the corridor, originally designed as a day room for the use of patients who were to reside in the rooms along the corridor, had to be used as a dormitory. In this room half of the patients slept. Thirty beds were side-by-side and

end-to-end in that area. There was just enough room between the beds to walk through. There was no place for a patient to keep personal possessions. Anything of value had to be kept locked in the office or kept on one's person.

I never could really understand it, but one thing stolen most frequently was Bibles. It seemed that no matter how many Bibles were given to patients it was only a matter of days before the Bibles would be stolen by another patient. How hungry these patients were for a salvation which never seemed to come!

At our afternoon seminar George tried to formulate the question.

"So what does salvation mean? I always thought it meant that people had to believe in something to be saved. That's what I preached all the time—if you believe everything will be O.K. 'All things work together for good' and all that. Now I don't know . . . what does it mean?" (He didn't address the question to anyone in particular.)

"I know what you mean, I didn't want to ever go back to that ward again after the first day." It was Adam. He actually had gone back, many times.

"I guess we really don't know what it means at all."

"Maybe that's why we're here, to find out."

"O.K. then, what is it?"

"No neat answer."

"Maybe it means something spiritual that happens inside."

"What does that mean?"

"I don't know."

"What could it mean to anybody if they were over there on that ward and couldn't get out, were robbed of personal dignity, didn't have any hope?"

"Maybe we're off on the wrong track."

"How's that?"

"Maybe we're asking the wrong question. I mean—who cares what a word means? So what? Does it help them over there if we decide what one of our words means?"

"But you can't say that salvation is meaningless; then the whole structure crumbles."

"Aw come off it, that's not what I said. Anyway, let the whole thing crumble if it doesn't mean anything."

"Hit me again with it then."

"What I'm saying is that we sit here talking about the meaning of a word, s-a-l-v-a-t-i-o-n, a *word*. How ridiculous can we get."

"Maybe we ought to be asking what we can *do*."

"That sounds good, but I don't know I really follow you."

"I mean, defining words don't help patients, what can we *do* for them. In other words I get the feeling that I'm like the Pharisee, you know, too busy with my prayers to notice the guy who's next to me."

"I guess that's something I never saw before. I was always so busy talking to people in my church that I didn't ever hear what they had to say or did anything for them."

". . . we all have sinned and come short of the glory of God . . ."

"Jeees, George, suddenly I feel like I like you. . . . You always came across to me as a real, well, funny guy. I never liked you."

"Yeah, I felt that too. I mean I wanted to be closer to all of you but I guess I was too much involved in who I was, or wasn't, or something. (long pause) I guess I never told you this before (addressing the group) but

I'm about to get kicked out of my church if I don't shape up." (tears)

"I don't know, I really appreciate what George said. I don't know, I guess I just feel lost, I mean . . . oh, I don't know what I mean." Mary Reynolds was struggling very hard.

"I guess I've been struggling to be one of the 'guys' but I've really been on the outside like George. But I couldn't let myself get close to him either."

"Why don't you go over and sit next to him then?"

"Do we have to stop now? It seems like we are just beginning to get somewhere."

Work
with
7 Relatives

Nearly every time you meet with relatives you have brought home to you the humanness of the situations which surround each patient, the intimate patterns of involvement which are part of each person's life. Life seems to get so infernally complicated at times.

There was a note under the door of the office. It said simply: "Chaplain, I've tried to see you several times but you don't seem to be in your office. Could I see you sometime soon? Jim Hunchfield, R. R. 3, New Ipswich."

You feel a little guilty, a little angry. You should have been in your office, you shouldn't have missed him. You tell yourself you can't be everywhere at the same time. It helps a little bit.

You check the records. Yes, there is a Mrs. Hunchfield who is here as a patient, admitted two days ago. You haven't seen her yet. (You're getting behind on your calling, *Chaplain*, better get with it!)

The record tells you that the patient has been hospitalized before, in fact on two different occasions. Hospitalizations have been about one year apart and for about two months on the first admission and four months on the second. Each time she has been diagnosed as "chronic undifferentiated schizophrenia."

Dr. Cohen explained on many occasions that schizophrenia was the catchall of mental disease. While there were clear symptoms and syndromes to be found in the Diagnostic and Statistical manual, people just didn't seem to follow the neat categories found there.

But whatever the label schizophrenia describes, it is cause for grave concern. Statistics vary considerably but some say that 40 percent of schizophrenia patients recover or improve, 80 percent of these within the first year, and with the chances of recovery decreasing with length of hospitalization. Sixty percent either fail to improve or simply suffer more or less permanent disintegration of personality.

How cold statistics are.

Jim Hunchfield wasn't a statistic. He was a big, beautiful human being, a bricklayer by trade.

"At first we had her in a private hospital. The psychiatrist said it was the best in this section of the country."

"When was that?"

"About ten years ago. It was just after the first baby was born. It was sort of like she came unglued. The doc said it was postpartum, or something like that. I really thought we had the thing licked. She came home and everything was great, really great. But a year or two later things started to go rotten again. I couldn't understand it, but she agreed to go back to the psychiatrist for regular sessions. It started costing thirty-five or forty dollars a week. My health insurance didn't cover it, so things were getting pretty rough. I don't know how to explain it, but as time went on she seemed to be getting worse rather than better. Why can't the docs level with you?"

"What happened?"

"It's hard to explain. Everything would seem to be fine—we used to go on picnics a lot, we seemed to have a lot of fun, I bought her everything for the house that she wanted. But it was like something was gnawing away at her inside. Things seemed to be fine, she might be standing at the sink doing dishes, and then for no reason at all she seemed to be a different person. She'd get a strange smile on her face and wouldn't respond when I'd talk to her. I'd ask her if anything was wrong and she'd just smile, and keep washing the dishes."

"What did you do?"

"I called the doc again. He said maybe she should be on some regular medication and to try to get her to come to see him. When I suggested she do it she smiled and said 'maybe, soon' or something like that. Then at other times she would admit maybe she really needed help and would do anything she could to make all of us happy. It was sort of like a roller coaster. One day she would be with it, the next day she wouldn't."

"That must have been pretty hard to take."

"I'm not the greatest one with words but it's gradually wore me down, kinda tore me apart inside too."

"Did the medication help?"

"Yeah, well sometimes, but then she didn't always take it. I'd catch her flushing it down the toilet, or throwing it in the trash. The doc said maybe she wouldn't have to be hospitalized again and recommended shock treatment in his office. She didn't go for that idea at all.

"I don't know how I got her there, but she did have

the shock in the office. That was rough. She would come home and couldn't seem to remember anything. I got really scared for what might happen to the kids, so I hired sort of a permanent babysitter for a while."

"Did she ever hurt the children?"

"No, I can't say she did. But it almost came to that. It's like a bad dream now, but one night I came home late, after dark—I'd been working out of town on a big job—and all the lights in the house were on, the doors were open, the TV blaring away, and I didn't see her or the kids anyplace.

"She was in the back driveway in the car with the kids. She had the doors locked. The oldest boy was in the back seat. He looked terrified. She was sitting in the front seat holding the youngest one very tightly, singing nursery rhymes. (heaves a big sigh) I felt sick all over. I tried to get her to unlook the doors but she wouldn't. I knew somethin' really had to be done so I called the doc over in Big City. He said there was nothing he could do, that we would have to try to get her to the hospital as soon as possible.

"By that time I knew she'd have to go to Smithville because I couldn't afford the private one anymore. So I called the state police and asked if they could help me.

"Yeah, it's like a nightmare, know what I mean? State police cars in the yard, neighbors peeking out their windows. God, I felt like dying. They took her away like some criminal, singing nursery rhymes. The kids were crying. Do you know what it's like, Chaplain, to have that happen to someone you love very much?"

"No, I don't, Jim."

"Then you can't understand what a hell it is. It's like the whole world just falls apart, you feel like shooting someone or something, but you don't know who or what."

"I guess only someone who has gone through it can know what it's like."

"I didn't see her for a week. When I did come here she cursed and screamed at me and told me to 'get my ass out of here' she never wanted to see me again. I couldn't believe this place. Compared to the private hospital this place is really, well, uh, I mean it just isn't the same.

"The kids are asking, well the older one did, when is Mommy coming home? Why does Mommy do such funny things? Do we have to make our beds while Mommy's gone? . . ."

The words keep coming and coming, you've heard almost identical words many times before, but every time you hear them they come at you as though they were new, and you know they have to come out.

"The next week she was all apologetic and said she wanted to love me forever, even tried to get me to go into her room so we could have sex, right here in the hospital.

"I'm sorry, Chaplain, I don't know why I'm telling you all this, but you can't tell just anybody, about some of these personal things, I mean."

"I understand." (It sounds almost hollow, useless, as you hear yourself saying it.)

"I got the idea for a while that it was something I did. The doc said maybe I ought to take her out more, he even made me think maybe there was something wrong with me. I thought maybe he was right. But it really didn't seem to matter, anything that I said or did." (long pause, you wait it out)

"So now she's here again, and I feel drained, completely drained, inside. I always thought of myself as a good man, not a real churchgoer, but I always tried to live by the Golden Rule. We always sent the kids to Sunday School, even went to church occasionally.

"Maybe at times you wonder how God could let things like this happen?" (Careful now, Chaplain, you're jumping ahead of him a bit, but it sounds like that's what he's getting at.)

"Yeah, I guess, but then I guess I don't know that much about religion. All I know is that everything is really all mixed up, crazy, yeah, crazy, and I don't know what to do."

"Who's taking care of the children?" (You really screwed up that time, Art. Here's a man in front of you searching to find some way out of his terribly tragic situation, he's practically begging for help, he's at the end of his rope, and all you can say is, "Who's taking care of the children?")

"Oh, my mother came over for a while. Chaplain, I know I can trust you, because you're a minister, but I've got to say this, I mean I wonder what you think about it. Well what I'm trying to say is I don't see how I can live with this woman any more, I've been thinking of divorcing her. I mean, uh, I love her, but I don't know how much I can take, and how much all of this is going to affect the kids. How much does a person have to take anyway?" (He's quite upset now, it's finally come out. Now you know why he stopped by your office. It took a long time to get to it, but even the way you screwed up didn't keep him from it.)

"You just don't see any other way out?" (Now that's a little better, encourage him to explore this further.)

"I don't know, I just don't know. I've thought and

I've thought. Sometimes I lay awake half of the night just thinking. What's marriage all about anyway? What's life all about anyway? It's sort of like at times it's some great tragedy, some conspiracy, even those you love turn against you, what you've always worked for. You don't get any answers from the docs. I mean they say this or that, but it doesn't answer your questions. They say, 'maybe she'll be O.K.', or 'there's another medication we haven't tried.' I don't know, I feel responsible for her, but do I have to ruin the rest of my life? And then there's the kids. I don't want to be selfish, and I'm not looking for another woman, but what do I do?"

Somehow you just don't feel you know how to answer these questions. You almost wish that someone would answer them for you. "You think maybe you ought to divorce her, but you aren't sure."

"Yeah, well, I don't really know. It's getting so I can't sleep good at night, I don't care if I go to work any more or not. I really want to do the best thing for her."

"What *is* the best thing for her?"

"I don't know, I thought maybe *you* could tell me, Chaplain."

"I wish I could tell you right this minute Jim, but I don't know either. I'd be glad to try to struggle with you though, to help you find the answer to that question."

"Well, I guess I was looking for an easy answer. But if anyone ought to know it ought to be me—there just aren't any easy answers, are there?"

"No, I don't think there are."

"I guess this whole business has mixed me up a lot.

Somehow I feel a little better now. Could I see you next week when I come to visit?"

"Sure, Jim."

You were tempted to give Jim Hunchfield some easy answers. You could have said: "The church has always taught that divorce is wrong," "You need more faith, I'm going to pray that God will give you the strength to bear your cross," or "The history of your wife's illness with continued hospitalization, etc., form a pattern which indicates very little chance of recovery. You'd better consider your own needs."

Just as you have learned that your students have to find their own answers, so you have learned that relatives have to find their own answers too. Of course they need help, but not the help of rigid, unfeeling, arbitrary authoritarianism with its advice far removed from the reality of life. They need someone who can stand with them, help them struggle, support, encourage, be with them, listen to them. If they take *your* answers then in that measure you rob them of the experience of being responsible for themselves.

This has been the first session with Jim Hunchfield. You don't know how his decision will come out.

Jim is just one husband, one relative. There are literally hundreds of others right now coming to Smithville State Hospital every week.

You do what you can, other staff members do what they can—everybody agrees it's not enough. Somehow with all our modern understanding of personality, in spite of all the good intentions of churches, civic organizations, political parties, in spite of all our talk of loving our neighbor, far too many people have to struggle with life and death issues alone.

Money goes to build roads rather than treatment

facilities. The means of healing are locked up in professionalism and come with a high price tag. Society doesn't teach people how to face the real problems of life. So much of the religions has become irrelevant to life.

There you go again, preaching sermons to yourself, Art King, sitting there daydreaming. You've got to get moving. You've got to see Mrs. Hunchfield, you've got to see the clinical director, you've got to get over to the staff meeting in "D" building, you've got to start working on next Sunday's sermon.

You've got to . . .

You've got to . . .

You've got to . . .

8 Preaching

Text: Luke 18:9-14

A work crew is busy moving back the basketball backstops, the gym floor is being swept, exercise apparatus is being moved back off the stage, time-honored wooden chairs are being set up on the floor—Smithville State Hospital is getting ready for religious services tomorrow.

The choir will spend most of Saturday evening rehearsing. No parish pastor could ask for a more dedicated choir. They aren't professionals by any means, but they sing with enthusiasm. (Somebody said that word means "God in us.")

Being in the choir at Smithville was a special honor. Since the number was limited to thirty, whenever a vacancy occurred patients almost literally fought to get in. (Not every parish church has that problem.) No one was concerned about whether he was "Protestant, Catholic, Jew, or none." These kinds of distinctions were much minimized at SSH—at least in the choir.

You arrive early on Sunday morning. For various reasons services here tend to be early on Sunday morning. For some reason they never have entrusted you with a key to the gymnasium. This morning it appears that the person responsible has overslept; at least he isn't here yet. You're locked out of your own church! Sure, some one will be along soon with a key, but it's the principle of the thing.

So you stand there pondering the irony and humor of it all. (Yes, the *humor*, don't ever let that get away from you.) They trust you with keys to everything else—the wards, other buildings, the staff rest rooms—but you can't get a key to your own church!

You chuckle a little bit to yourself, you know the background of this particular situation. Another example of the "humanness" of even professional staff members. Another example of "he who has the keys has the power." Right now *you're* powerless, you get a little bit of the feeling of what it's like for patients behind those locked doors.

That's *good*, it will help you preach with a little more humility this morning.

"Good morning, Reverend King, I'm so sorry you have to stand outside waiting like this, but there's nothing I can do . . ."

It is Mrs. Olsen, choir director. She has a key.

"Good morning, Mrs. Olsen, sure am glad to see you."

You are too. Mrs. Olsen is typical of the kind of employee that keeps SSH running. She is intensely dedicated to the patients, she feels she has a "calling" here. Being a very talented person she could easily make more money elsewhere, but she insists making money isn't her goal in life. She's where she wants to be. She has a way of handling the choir you're sure few people could duplicate.

The patients begin arriving for the service. They come in groups. You can tell which wards or buildings are coming. The choir is running through the music one final time—sounds especially good this morning (some mornings it doesn't).

Building "H" hasn't arrived yet and it is nearly time to begin. Must be short on help this morning with no one to bring the patients. Maybe a phone call to the nursing supervisor would help. Or it might only aggravate the situation—"The chaplain called *demanding* the patients for the service." "We do the best we can, doesn't he realize that?"

It's rather amazing to see the number of people in the congregation this morning. The female side is full, the male side over half full. You feel uncomfortable about that, having to see the men and women segregated. It's like a flashback in church history. But you're told it "has to be that way," because "bad things would happen if you let them sit together." You wonder what "bad things" would happen right there in the church service.

The service has just begun and you are reading the responsive reading as you become aware of some kind of commotion in the congregation. You see two psychiatric aides coming down a side aisle. No one pays much attention. The responsive reading goes on.

"Yea, though I walk through the valley of the shadow of death. . . "

At last you catch a glimpse and recognize that Suzie has had another seizure. She is an epileptic who is having a great deal of difficulty controlling her seizures.

For some reason they seem to come during church more than anywhere else. You wonder . . .

Everybody wonders, nobody seems to know what to do about it.

The scripture this morning is Luke 18:9-14. Just as the reading begins the patients from "H" building arrive. Probably it is just as well you didn't call, they probably *were* doing the best they could. But it does tend to disrupt the service.

Services here at the hospital tend to be shorter than those on the "outside," particularly the sermon. You sometimes jokingly tell people in the community they should visit the services here once in a while "because the sermons are short and there is no offering." They usually say "great," but never come.

As the choir sings you look out across the faces of the congregation. They look attentive, entranced, expectant, worshipful (well mostly). Some patients are dressed in "their Sunday best." Others have on overalls or cotton dresses. One has on only a T-shirt, faded blue jeans and a pair of tennis shoes.

Many times as you have moved about the "outside" church community you've had people question you about the meaningfulness of these services. One well-meaning deacon once got you in a corner and said, *very* seriously, "Chaplain King, what do *those people* get out of a worship service?" You remember too your spontaneous reply. "Deacon Jones, what do *you* get out of a worship service?" That had turned out to be an interesting conversation.

Now it's time for the sermon. They always turn the lights down in the gymnasium when the sermon begins. (Maybe that's when they expect the "bad things" to happen.) Now you're literally in the spotlight.

"The Pharisee thought he was something he wasn't."

Heads nod in the affirmative.

"The Publican didn't try to be something he wasn't, he knew what he was—and he sought God's mercy."

"Amen, that's true. . . ."

One thing you like about this congregation is that they *respond*. "Outside" as you preach to a congregation you are usually greeted by dead silence. Expressionless faces stare at you. No one dares respond in any verbal or even nonverbal way during the sermon.

You've also had people ask, "But don't they disrupt the services sometimes?"

"Of course they do. But it's O.K."

Now the sermon is nearly finished.

"Honesty in confronting ourselves is very important. . . ."

You've been noticing a man standing up occasionally in back, now he walks down the center aisle and stands in front of you. What do you do? You stop, bend down and ask him what he wants.

He says, "May I sing the Lord's Prayer now?"

You say, "No, I don't think this would be a good time."

He says, "O.K." and walks back up the aisle. Try to catch him later. Find out what's going on, how you can help.

"Our lives are never enhanced by pretending to be something we're not, or in denying what we actually are."

"Yeh. . . . true. Amen. . . ."

"Yet there is a great danger here."

"Danger, great danger." You seem to have an echo out there, but that's O.K. You know someone is *hearing* you.

"By focusing too long and too hard on our shortcomings we can lose perspective. All too often around here I see people who have become preoccupied with their shortcomings. These people cut themselves off from the good life by continually berating themselves."

Some one in the front row is now on his knees in an attitude of prayer. Someone behind him looks like he is asleep, but you can't tell because the lights are so dim. You'd better suggest that they not turn the lights down quite so low next Sunday.

"How badly many people treat themselves! They treat themselves much worse than they would ever dream of treating others.

"One thing that stands out clearly from the life and teachings of Jesus Christ is his attitude of love toward persons.

"He knew what people were like—He really knew!"

"Yes, Lord, Amen. Uh-huh."

"Yet he proclaimed forgiveness, the possibility of a new life, and he lived a life of love for persons.

"If Jesus felt this way, then how important it is for us to be willing to forgive ourselves and treat ourselves with all the respect due us as the unique persons we are."

Then the clapping begins—there is applause from the congregation! That happens every once in a while. You can't predict when it may happen, it just does. You can't imagine it happening "outside."

Greeting people at the "door" in the gymnasium is a little difficult as there are three doors in use each morning after the service. You usually alternate doors, greeting people at a different door each Sunday.

They have to stay with their group. They always go out the same door.

Some people avoid you.

Some people squeeze your hand so hard they almost crush it.

One woman hugs you. She has a strange look in her eye.

Some say, "That was a fine sermon, Reverend." You wonder what that means.

You notice a woman holding back, waiting for the crowd to thin out a bit. She works her way over to you. She looks familiar, but you aren't sure, there are so many.

"I want to tell you I enjoyed your sermon." It's a pretty stock comment but you notice that there are tears in her eyes. She's trying to tell you something. What is it, how can you best handle this?

"What did you *think* about the sermon?" (That didn't seem like the best thing to say, but nothing else seemed to come at the moment, and you sort of had to say something.)

"What you said was true of me."

"Oh?"

"For so long I've not been able to forgive myself for what I have done. . . ."

The counseling was beginning right there but it would have to be continued later. You get her name and ask to see her tomorrow.

What happened?

Subsequent counseling sessions with this person indicated that the sermon, the "proclamation" from the pulpit, the redeeming declaration from the context of the divine service, was serving as a turning point in this person's life. This person who had been lost in a morass of self-condemnation and lost from the community of persons, was beginning the long trip back to community, back to a sense of personal integrity. In short, she was beginning to find salvation from the lostness of condemnation and alienation.

Now, who was that fellow who asked if he could sing the Lord's Prayer? Maybe Mrs. Olsen will know.

But you have to hurry out now, you're preaching over in Beach City to a small church.

You won't be back at SSH today. You should be, to see relatives who come a long way and find it difficult to come any other day but Sunday.

But you promised the afternoon to yourself and your family. After all, you have to keep your "mental health" too.

The
9 Mentally
Retarded

Smithville State Hospital had a rather large popula-
tion of mentally retarded persons. Perhaps the term
"exceptional persons" would be better. The trouble
with any descriptive words or phrase of this kind is
that it is intended to convey some special meaning, but
after a while the special meaning gets lost and then a
new phrase has to be found.

These people are "exceptional," they are different,
they demolish our cherished ideas of what it means,
basically, to be a person. They teach us something
about the nature of interpersonal relationships. They
challenge our wordy theologies.

Because there was no place else to go, these people
had begun to come to Smithville—"Out of sight, out of
mind." "They can't have a 'normal' life anyway." You
ask yourself, "what is a 'normal' life?" and you get a
lot of interesting answers to that one. Sometimes it
seems like only a person who can "hack it" in a highly
competitive society is considered "normal." Just *being*

a person doesn't seem to count for much more some times.

Watch it, your anger isn't helping anybody, *Chaplain*. Channel some of that thought and energy into some constructive action.

It is interesting that the clergy seem more interested in the mentally retarded than the mentally ill. Maybe it's less threatening. You've heard more than one say "at times I've wondered if I might end up here" (with the mentally ill). But you almost never hear them say, "At times I wonder if I might be mentally retarded." Yet to an extent and by definition we all share in both these conditions.

Dr. E. Woodruff Ribicoff is speaking. "So you see when we speak of mental subnormality, of mental retardation, we note that there are three main themes: the biological, the psychological, and the cultural."

"Woody" Ribicoff, as he is known to his colleagues on the staff, is a physician who seems to have "come into his own" in working with the mentally retarded. He is the mainstay of the training program for the clergy, and he never tires of lecturing to them. He's an enjoyable lecturer. He knows his material forward and backward and seems to have some deeply personal thing which motivates him in this work. You've never figured out what it is. What difference would it make if you knew? About the only thing you object to is at times he is very authoritarian and seems to intimidate some clergy.

"But, Doctor, we try to include them, but they don't fit in our Sunday School." It was a minister from a nearby church speaking, a regular member of the clergy group. "But they just don't seem to fit."

"What do you mean, how don't they fit?"

"Well, we have one fellow whose mother was told by the doctors that he was considered a six-year-old . . ."

"How old is he?"

"Well he's fifteen, chronologically, but small for his age. But since he's six mentally we obviously put him in the six-year-old class. But it just doesn't work."

"Then, Reverend, it would appear that there is your problem. You have someone who emotionally is a teen-ager, but you put him with six-year-olds."

"Oh . . . well, what do we do then? I mean, what kind of curriculum could we use for such people?" (I can see he's uncomfortable and he's trying to get out of it by putting Woody on the spot.)

"Let's see what kind of experiences some of the rest of the group have had, and how they have handled it."

Woody was good that way, he knew how to handle groups, especially clergy—well, most of the time.

I met Woody in the washroom later that morning. "I think the clergy are a little afraid of you at times, Woody."

"That's O.K., Reverend, as long as it helps them to learn about the retarded."

I don't know why, he never would call me "Art." Maybe he always secretly wanted to be a minister, he seemed to like the word Reverend so much.

Training the clergy was the easy part. It doesn't confront you directly with some of the "human" issues in a face-to-face way.

"Chaplain King?"

"Yes, you must be Mr. Channing, and this is Mrs. Channing. How do you do."

"And this is George."

"How do you do, George."

"Mmmmm Hwww, howw doo."

It was uncanny. George Jr., aged 35, was startlingly similar in appearance to his father George Sr., aged 68. If he were not a mongoloid (Woody always preferred the term Down's Syndrome) he would almost be his father's twin, only considerably shorter. He was dressed in a well-fitting suit with white shirt and tie.

George Jr. held out a short, thick hand but didn't respond to my handshake. He had the slanting eyes, the rather awkward appearance so characteristic of those with Down's Syndrome—flat nose, surprisingly little hair on his head.

"Georgie wanted to come down and see the new place where he will be living." Mrs. Channing looked a little bit uneasy, to say the least.

Woody took Mrs. Channing and Georgie for a "tour" of his new home. Mr. Channing wanted to talk.

Georgie had been most fortunate in his experience at home. He had always been loved, went with the family to church. He did reasonably well with table manners and often went with the family to restaurants. A great deal of his time at home was spent "writing." He couldn't really write, but he spent a great deal of time neatly scribbling on writing tablets. He also spent quite a bit of time in front of the television set, but got regular exercise. Mr. Channing knew from the time Georgie was born that there was no cure known for his son's condition. He was more fortunate (or smarter) than some—instead of spending unreal sums of money for hoped-for cures, he spent it making a good life for Georgie.

"But you see, Chaplain, I'm retired now and Georgie has lived much longer than I anticipated he would. He does have some physical problems, but it looks like he'll live longer than we will."

You can almost quote to him what he'll say next.

"So my wife and I realize we won't be around forever, so we thought the time had finally come when we had to bring Georgie here so we'd know he'd be taken care of. There seems no alternative at this point."

Mr. Channing is also an "exceptional" person. He's doing what's best for his son, as he sees it. He's lived with this situation all his life. Now he has to take the last step. He handles it well.

"My wife's not taking it too well, he's still her little little boy, you know . . . and maybe it sounds a little selfish, but we also think since we're retired now and getting older, that we'd like to do a little traveling, and some of the things we've never really been able to do."

Mr. Channing isn't asking for advice, but he needs to explain, he needs to make clear his motivation. He isn't "dumping" Georgie on the hospital, he is taking the only next step he knows.

No one knows another alternative at this point. A private hospital would certainly be better in terms of physical surroundings, patient-staff ratio, etc., but Mr. Channing can't afford that.

"We looked for a long time for a family that might take him in, but there just aren't any."

You can almost feel the gloom descending on the staff meeting. Georgie has just been discussed and admitted to SSH.

"How can we give adequate care to this kind of patient?" "We just don't have the staff." Mr. Davenport isn't very enthusiastic today, and with good reason.

"They have more physical problems than other patients, we'll have to have more medical and nursing staff."

"We asked for more staff from the last legislature but they turned us down."

Woody isn't letting the gloom settle on him. "O.K., O.K., it means we've got to do some planning, we've got to find ways."

"What do you suggest?"

"Well first we've got to *want* to do it. That's the key. We've got to *really* want to."

"It's time we began working and planning with the Association for Retarded Children."

"Aren't there some Sunday School things you can do with these people, Reverend?"

"I've started making some plans. I'll be glad to share them at the next staff meeting."

"Another thing we've got to face is the 'crib cases.' Nobody wants to work over there." Mrs. Short, director of nursing, raises a loaded issue.

In "F" building there are over one hundred patients who are totally incapable of caring for themselves. Not too long ago these people would have survived only a very short time. But with modern antibiotics and other advances in the medical sciences they are living longer. Most of them have to be kept in beds with high railings so they won't fall out, hence the term "crib cases."

It takes mature people, dedicated people, to work with this kind of patient. Not everyone can do it. Not everyone can even afford to work there because the wages are extremely low. The work is *very* demanding, *very* emotionally draining. Mrs. Short certainly does have something to worry about.

"And we're going to be getting more. They're going to start piling up!"

"We'll find a way, we *will*. Mrs. Short, I want you to prepare a list of the positions you need and a statement outlining your problems over there. Have it in my office the day after tomorrow."

Back in your office you start thinking about how you fit into all this.

You've got to come up with a religious education program. Not for the "crib cases," but for the trainable and educable groups.

You've got to find ways to be more supportive of the staff; Woody's doing a better job of that than you are.

You've got to spend more time with the relatives of these patients. You've done almost nothing there. Maybe a letter to all of them, or . . .

You've got to wrestle with some of the theological questions the clergy have been raising.

You've got to be sure to see Georgie tomorrow.

A lot seems to happen in one day.

An Interview with
10 Jesus Christ

"It has been a long time since I have seen a classic religious delusion." It was a psychiatrist from a nearby hospital speaking to a group of ministers and priests.

This had not been my experience. For a number of years I had been intrigued with the variety of religious delusions and religious ideology with which I had been confronted as a mental hospital chaplain.

Whether or not you get to such personal things as religious views, or even uncover religious ideations which are bizarre depends a lot on what you ask and who you are. But not always. Sometimes such symptomatology is so strong that it breaks forth and nothing could cover it up.

Take the case of John F. John always had been considered a little different from others. Kept to himself a lot. Talked about things most other people couldn't understand. He wasn't in any real difficulty, though, until he decided that God had called him to be an apostle and he took off his shoes and started down the

79

road following the Lord's voice. On the route of his apostleship he stopped by the fields and "gleaned" for his food in the good old biblical way. Some owners of gardens along his way seemed to object, and before long John found himself at Smithville State Hospital. When he got talking to some of the social workers and psychiatrists—when he found people who said they were interested in what he thought—he "let it all hang out." John has been at SSH for over seven years now. He's a good worker on the farm, but he complains at times about not being let go to pursue his apostleship. He still sees all kinds of fascinating visions and "openings" of a religious nature. He shares them freely with the chaplain, but with few others. No medication that he has received since he has been at the hospital seems to have had much of any effect on him. If one could imagine how one of the prophets of old might have looked, and acted, one might have some idea of the appearance of John F.

These religious delusions come in all varieties. For me, one of the most bizarre was the seventy-year-old lady on one of the wards who, when I would say hello to her, would smile and ask me to come closer. When I would do this she would pat her stomach and say "I have a Jesus baby in here, he will be born very soon now."

Then there was the man who had been committed to the hospital by the court. He was taking a correspondence Bible-study course and insisted he was going to become a "preacher" when he got out. He had been sentenced for an indefinite term in our hospital because he had raped several young girls and nearly killed another—in addition to such other relatively less serious activities as breaking-and-entering, and forgery. Actually I think he sensed his need and was trying to find through his study of the Bible the necessary "limits" for his behavior. Well, wasn't the apostle Paul "the chief of sinners"?

It's hard to forget the young lady who announced one day to you that she was God. She explained it this way. "Right at the present time I am a woman, in a woman's body, but I am in the process of metamorphosis. I will soon have the male organs and then I will be Jesus. When I am Jesus then I will be God."

Most people on the staff were really afraid of this kind of thing. When this sort of thing would come in group therapy sessions Mr. Davenport, the psychologist, would say, "We don't talk about religion here, why don't you talk about that with the chaplain." It got so after a while there were so many patients with "this kind of thing" that wasn't talked about in group therapy that the priest and I formed our own "religious therapy" group for them. In this group they could talk about their values and ideals, their understanding and misunderstanding of the Bible, their hopes, fears, loves, heaven, hell, etc.

Jesus Christ became part of this group.

"Chaplain King?"

"Yes."

"This is Mrs. Krueger on Ward II and I think we have a patient here you want to see." Mrs. Krueger had been working with me in helping to spot patients with religious symptomatology.

"Hello, I'm Art King."

At first he didn't respond at all.

"I'm a chaplain here."

"A . . . chaplain . . ."

"A minister on the staff of the hospital."

"I'm Jesus Christ." That was all he said. He walked away.

I went to the nursing station and chatted with Mrs. Krueger. She said that he had been brought in last night by the police. The brief admission note by the admitting physician said that he had been apprehended by the police at a factory in a nearby city where he was talking all kinds of "crazy" talk. The owner of the factory said he had a history of being in the hospital, so the police simply brought him straight to SSH. There was nothing to indicate anything religious in the note at all.

Mrs. Krueger said that since he came in he had said almost nothing, except when asked his name he insisted that he was Jesus Christ. He was also quite agitated and had been put on rather high dosages of Thorazine to slow him down. She said the medication had already begun to have some effect.

For some time I had hoped to be able to make tape recordings of some of these classic delusions, but I had not been successful. I had hoped to be able to do some serious research in regard to them. As I tried to "capture" them I began to see why so little had been done in this area. They are extremely difficult to capture. These delusions are elusive, extremely difficult to understand, often contradictory, hopelessly inconsistent, and often *very* private.

Jesus Christ was not going to be interviewed. He steadfastly refused. After about six weeks, however, I was surprised to look up and find someone at my office door—it was "Jesus."

"Reverend?"

"Yes, hello, come in." (Said somewhat dumbfoundedly.)

"Mr. Davenport said you had a religious group that maybe I could be part of."

"Yes, we'd be glad to have you. Won't you come in for a minute so we can talk about it."

Patients can be rather hard on each other at times. Usually it's good therapy. At first "Jesus" couldn't easily take jokes about his thinking he was "Christ." But he learned to step back a little and look at himself. From the religious therapy group he was told, many, many times, that Jesus was a special person in church history which the church has considered divine, so he couldn't be Jesus. From the group therapy led by the psychologist he learned that he had been "sick." Finally these two things fit together for him.

About four weeks later the staff felt he was ready to go. He was far from "well," but it was felt he could make no further progress at SSH, and that he should be discharged and referred to a mental health clinic in his own city.

On an impulse I stopped by his ward and asked him if he would be willing to be interviewed and talk about the ideas he had about being Jesus and what it had meant to him.

"I'd be most happy to, Reverend, if you think it'll help anyone else."

"When I came in, I thought I was . . . Jesus, of course. But the main thing is I had a hatred for another religion. Like I had a hatred for the Catholics, and I . . . thought I had come in a revelation, you know, (like) in the Book of Revelation, I thought I had returned. Well I thought I was in the flesh and people were telling me that I was Jesus. And I was out on the streets, parading around the streets. And I was—and I felt my mind was open, for one thing. I thought my mind was open and everyone could hear my thoughts."

In this initial stage in which he believed he was Jesus he felt that he had a special mission and that he had special powers.

He continued, "I thought I had special powers. Like when I was at work, I felt something snap in my head. I mean I thought, I thought it was something above. I guess something snapped in my head and—'cause I was ready to—was going to kill the Catholics, kill the nuns and priests. I had thought—I thought the Catholics had to do with it because they were witches and warlocks, you know, because I saw on the street they looked like witches, you know? . . . My mission was to destroy nuns and priests, because the end was coming, fire and brimstone, you know? So I thought I was going to have to burn all the buildings down, the churches down. You see, everything had to be burned, see? . . ."

You can't help but remember the case of another man who thought the communists were coming and who killed his daughters so the communists wouldn't rape them. Fortunately "Jesus" hadn't killed anyone.

He had stopped by the place where he had worked to pick up his paycheck to buy groceries for the "last meal" before carrying out his "mission." Fortunately for him, and for other people, his bizarre behavior was spotted there and the police were summoned and subsequently brought him to the hospital.

Since being in the hospital, he had been able to gain insight into his own bizarre thinking. He attributed his insight basically to the medication which "helped him slow down" and also to his own searching of the Bible. As he began to recover from the delusion that he was Christ (he used the names Jesus and Christ interchangeably) he made an interesting transition on the way to recovering his own identity. From believing himself to be Christ he moved to believing he must have been a "false Christ."

He said, "Yes, I was really convinced . . . (that he was Jesus) but yet I hadn't read the Bible. If I would have read it, I would have seen with my own eyes that ah—that ah—he was supposed to come in the sky or something like that . . . but maybe I—but after it was all over, I thought—I knew I wasn't Jesus, I began to think I was one of the false Jesuses. You know, like you said in the Bible, it would be false Christ?"

Then came the time when he could say, "I was sick." When he came to see he was neither Christ nor false Christ. When he could say, "I didn't understand the Bible very well, I appreciate your help in getting it straight."

There was a time in church history when anyone who claimed to be Jesus Christ was brutally tortured and killed by representatives of the church. In the name of love and for the good of the kingdom of God thousands upon thousands of men, women, and even children were slaughtered because they exhibited behavior different from "normal" people.

We have come a long way indeed!

11 Death

"*Reverend* King?"

"Yes, Woody?"

"Yes, could you meet me down at the morgue?"

"Sure, what's up?" Sure wish he would call me "Art," or at least *chaplain*, or even chaplin.

"We have a body down there and I want to talk to you about it. I'll explain when I meet you."

"O.K."

It was just this morning that Woody had presented and discussed a film showing an autopsy with a CPE group. There must be a connection here.

There had been quite a bit of discussion about the film. Woody and I agreed it would be good for the students to have this kind of experience. If these men were going to be parish pastors, if they were to do their work knowledgeably, they needed a broad exposure to the "realities" of life and death.

Death certainly is a "reality." In a psychiatric hospital death is seldom talked about, except in relation to patients who are considered a high suicidal risk.

But death was more frequent than most people on the "outside" might realize. The chaplain had the task of notifying patients when their family or friends at home died. By way of contrast, it was usually the medical staff of the hospital who notified families when patients died. It wasn't clear why this was so, except that they had the legal responsibility.

Now you're down at the morgue.

"Come in, come in, close the door."

"What's happening?"

"Well we have this fellow here, died the other day, and he has no family, friends, literally no one, he was over in 'A' building for years. Anyway we have all the paperwork done to send him down to the med school. . ."

"Yes. . . ." He's trying to tell you something but doesn't seem to be doing too well. This isn't like Woody.

"O.K. O.K., it's just that talking to all you clergy about the autopsy business and all got me thinking: Maybe you'd like to say some prayers or something over this guy before we send him down."

You answer much too quickly. "No, I don't think I'd like to." Then you add insult to injury. "Maybe *you* feel like *you*'d like to say some prayers or something." Well, O.K., now it's out.

Woody explodes.

"No, dammit, I don't want to do it, but it seems to me that somebody ought to. I'm just a medical man, we don't like to face death, but when you've had hell in life like this guy had, and you end up in this place, and you have no relatives, no friends, nothing, and then they hack you like a piece of meat, it just seems like somebody, somehow ought to take the time to say something, to add just a little dignity to your life, and if you don't do it, *Chaplain*, who will?"

Wow!

"Why don't we go get a cup of coffee and talk about it, Woody. Frankly, I don't feel altogether comfortable here myself."

We got our coffee and took it up to Woody's office. It looked more like a professor's office than a physician's. More books than any other office in the hospital.

"The reason I kind of turned this back to you, Woody, was that my own particular denomination has never felt there was anything magical about saying prayers or reading services over a dead body, when there's no one around to hear them."

"Yes, I know, and I guess I agree with you. It's just how I *feel* about it."

"I know, and I appreciate the fact you shared that feeling with me. Not many physicians would do that."

"It's just that it's like it's the last indignity that an uncaring society can inflict on a person. I know it doesn't make sense to want to say something nice over a corpse, but I guess I'm perhaps influenced by my own religious background more than I am aware at times."

"How's that?"

"Just between you and me, *Reverend*, I always really wanted to be a rabbi. My mother was dead set against it, though."

"Please call me Art, I've wanted to ask you that for a long time."

"O.K., O.K. So now you know my secret. I'm a frustrated clergyman myself."

"Did I ever tell you I wanted to be a physician but couldn't afford it?"

The laughter must have echoed through all the corridors and buildings of SSH!

At 5:45 P.M. a strange scene took place in the morgue. A would-be "rabbi" and a would-be "physician" read prayers and scriptures over the body of one of the "meekest of the earth." A short sermon was preached on the dignity of life, and its sacredness. The body was committed to its eternal rest. And the "cooler" door was shut!

Beautiful.

Beautiful.

For you the subject was over, closed—but not for the students. They didn't have the input you did yesterday. You let them go ahead and work on it.

"All the time I was watching that film I had the feeling it was really me there."

"Made you feel uncomfortable?"

"That's not the word for it—I don't know how to describe it."

"All I kept thinking about was my father. They did an autopsy on him when he died last year. They said something about taking some organs out or something —but I never knew it was like *that!*"

"How do we separate the body and the soul, or spirit? You get so used to thinking of a person in terms of his body. It's hard to shift gears. But the person really isn't his body, is he?"

"Would you want an autopsy done on *your* father?"

"I guess I'd really have to think about that awhile, I'm not sure. It's easy enough to *say* that man is really spirit, but . . ."

"Well, what bothers me is a person dying in a place like this. I mean, you know, if someone's 'outside' you can kinda say, well, he lived a good long life, or he had a bad accident, or something—but he at least was *living*. But here . . ."

"But here what?"

"Well what I mean is here it's like a person hasn't been punished enough. His life isn't tragic enough—you've got to take away his last bit of dignity he has."

"You mean if you do an autopsy here?"

"Yeah."

"What would you do? I mean, we'll make you the superintendent here. Will you make a rule that no patient can die here?"

So, they're working on this "hard reality." It isn't easy. There aren't any textbook answers.

You don't try to reduce experience to the receding minima of conclusions. You let experience carry you on to expanding avenues of awareness, meaning. It's a long process. You never really sort it all out. Maybe when they go back for their final year of theological training . . . Maybe.

There is a special problem with the "crib cases" at SSH. Essentially it's a moral question.

Woody used to want to turn it over to you. "I'm bound to do everything I can to prolong the life of my patients. But how do I decide where even this approach stops? When do I pull out the IV's, etc. It seems to me that it's *your* problem—it's in the religious area."

That always makes you feel uncomfortable. It would be easy to make arbitrary decisions—great to play God. You might be God, but you don't have any legal responsibility. Woody does. You don't envy him at all! Yet it's your problem too.

There is an unexpected death at the hospital. It's Georgie. He'd been on the wards in "D" building for a while, but a week ago he had been placed on the medical ward. His many problems, particularly his diabetic condition, seemed to suddenly get out of hand. It appeared the diabetic condition caused his death. State law required an autopsy.

The hard thing to take about this was the fact that you had watched Georgie slowly go downhill after he came to SSH. Shortly after he came his parents went on an extended trip, were gone several months. Gradually you watched this well-mannered, neatly dressed person become a troublesome "retardate" dressed in "state" clothes.

The staff just didn't have the time to spend with Georgie. He was miserable. When his parents visited, it only seemed to make the situation worse. For a while it looked like he was making progress in his adjustment. Then his physical problems flared up. Woody was taking care of him. He was as surprised as anyone when Georgie suddenly died. Regardless of what the autopsy report says, you diagnose this one as "love deprivation."

The myth about death for you is related to the idea of living a long, full life. You expect to leave behind grandchildren and some happy memories in the hearts and minds of those who love you and know you. Life should be a happy experience, its end should be a fulfillment.

You just open the office door as you hear your phone ringing.

"Chaplain King."

"Yes, Chaplain, Mr. Johnson is dying, Ward 2A. There's no family we know about. Would you come over please."

You suspect there's nothing you can do. But don't forget what you always tell your students. "Maybe it's what you are more than what you can *do*."

You've faced this situation many times before. The record tells you: "Mr. Edgar Brown Johnson, Protestant, age 78, admitted to SSH forty years ago. Diagnosis: chronic schizophrenia, paranoid type. High school education, parents died when patient was a child, no known relatives living. No visitors for past five years."

"Mr. Johnson, I'm Chaplain King."

"Mr. Johnson hasn't spoken since they sent him over here. They should have sent him here before (to the medical ward). Poor man, he's been very sick."

Does Mr. Johnson hear?

Does he see?

Does he respond in any way?

Will he think you've come to give him the "last rites"?

You sense the sincere concern of the staff on the medical ward. At least he has *that*.

"Dr. Ribicoff said it would probably be only a matter of a few hours."

You do wish they wouldn't say it right in front of the patient. But, who's to say, maybe it's better that way, no secrets.

"Mr. Johnson, I'd like to share the Lord's Prayer with you."

"Our Father . . . " You notice that two members of the staff bowed their heads.

When there is no one to claim the body it is given the simplest burial possible. The local funeral director always calls and asks you if you will conduct a service.

"Will anyone be there?" You don't expect that there will be, but you ask anyway.

"No one but you and I, Reverend."

You dread this type of funeral service in a way, and

yet in another way it's always a good experience for *you*.

Woody's right, it doesn't seem proper that such a person's dignity not be enhanced at the end of his days.

The chairs are empty, but somehow it doesn't seem to matter. It somehow has to be said. You've often heard it said, "The funeral is for the mourners." True, but when there are no mourners? What then?

Maybe that's what you feel, Chaplain Arthur King, you feel you're the mourners, somehow in some small way you make up for the family and friends that aren't there, for the society that doesn't care.

It doesn't make *sense* (a deceptive word). Of course it doesn't—it's something you *feel*. And you've learned to trust your feelings.

Maybe on that lonely hillside you are merely talking to the wind.

It somehow meets *your* need. You don't have to answer to anybody for that.

So, What Is a Chaplain Anyway?

12

The morning walk to the mail room yields a letter from your denominational headquarters. This isn't too unusual since you're used to getting a lot of "junk mail" from there that doesn't have anything to do with your work. But this one is different, the address has been typed. You'd probably better read this one.

Well, what do you know. They want to know "what *is* a chaplain anyway?" You thought they'd never ask. Seriously now, they want to know if you will prepare a paper for a national meeting of ministers. So what happened? They at last recognized your greatness? Or did they run out of speakers and had to fill in at the last minute?

Of course you can't pass up such a "call from on high," so you get to work. Being the compulsive type at times you go in your office, lock the door, refuse to answer the phone, ignore all meetings, and revel in the luxury of spending the whole day if necessary trying to prepare something about the role of the chaplin (sure don't want to lose your sense of humor today).

Probably you should begin by pointing out that chaplaincies, as we see them today, are really a phenomenon of the past few decades of the present century. You are, or at least hope you are, the embodiment of the concern of the modern church for the healing of persons. (Sounds kind of pretentious, maybe it's what you like to be rather than what you are.)

You are one of a group of highly specialized and thoroughly trained clergy whose parishes are the health and welfare institutions of society. (Thorough training is right, you still get unbelievable looks when you say you have eight years of graduate study plus clinical training.)

O.K. Where do we go from here? Think, Chaplin! "Hmm. Well . . . uh."

Let's point out that there has been quite a bit of research on the chaplain's role. One of the first studies done by Gynther and Kempson showed that the staff at one of the big state hospitals down in South Carolina saw chaplains primarily as counselors, but they were seen as "preachers" by the patients. That's kind of interesting. The staff there also didn't think that education, administration, or evangelism were particularly important as part of the chaplain's work. Another thing that should be pointed out is that there also were considerable differences found in how various staff groups saw the chaplains. Nurses weren't very favorably disposed to chaplains, whereas psychiatric aides were; physicians and medical auxiliary were sort of "so-so." Gynther and Kempson didn't think that the staff really understood what the objectives or goals of the chaplain's program really were. You know that feeling pretty well, *Chaplain* King.

We shouldn't forget to mention also that another important thing found in that study was that people tended to look at the work of chaplains favorably if they themselves were "religious." Staff members who weren't themselves "religious" tended to downgrade the chaplain's work. That's an interesting point—it means that the staff has to be careful lest it project its own religious needs, or lack of them onto the patients. How can we be objective about the religious needs of patients?

A little while after that study another was done by Knights and Kramer in Cleveland, Ohio. They studied attitudes about what chaplains did. That was kind of interesting too. They found that almost all staff and patients agreed that chaplains ought to conduct worship and visit patients. That's not much of a surprise, and very, very traditional. Sacraments were also seen as pretty important there too. They also found that the medical staff was terribly traditional in their view of what chaplains did, and not especially appreciative of even those traditional functions. You always thought so, now it's "documented." (That makes it a lot more impressive, doesn't it?)

In these studies and others like them you begin to see that the bulk of the work done by chaplains today is really of a pretty non-traditional nature, and not appreciated much.

"What can we say about this? ..."

Let's sort out these non-traditional role-functions into three categories: teaching and research, administration, and therapy.

We might point out that teaching of other professionals and also research are certainly in one sense "non-traditional." That is, they aren't typical functions of the typical parish pastor. That's probably part of the problem; most people still apparently have the parish minister as the "model" when they think about what chaplain ought to be doing.

Is that beginning to change?

Careful, though, this might come across as sounding like you thought you were something "better" than a parish pastor. Just try to say, in as nonthreatening way as you can, that you are just a specialist, like in medicine for example.

All of us tend to lose perspective. There are many illustrations from the history of ministry of innovative types of ministry. (You'd better footnote a few of these in case someone wants to know "where to find it.") Anyway today there are so many innovations—lots of really exciting things going on.

Research—that's a little more difficult. Research has become such a highly specialized "science" these days. But you see that as part of your job as it ought to be of any pastor. Gathering information to restudy and interpret, utilizing some help from statistics. Sometimes the psychologists seem to think they invented research. Some chaplains even specialize in a research ministry. There can be a good case made for this. We've sure got to know a lot of things about ministry we don't know now if we are going to render pastoral care with the kind of professionalism that the importance of the task deserves.

Better be careful of the word professionalism, though—that's a red flag for some of your colleagues. Explain the way you use it carefully!

Anton Boisen, founder of the mental hospital chaplaincy, was a real research pioneer too. You'd better make a reference to him. Wonder why we haven't done more with this lead he gave us? We talk about it a lot, but don't seem to do too much about it.

Next, administrative duties, better say something about that. It works you up a bit, doesn't it, Chaplain King? You've never been able to understand quite why, but even many of your sophisticated fellow staff members seem to think that you somehow magically, without the use of time or any kind of secretarial assistance, somehow manage to answer correspondence, maintain files, make appointments, answer the phone, plan religious education programs, work on community projects with local clergy, plan and conduct programs of clinical pastoral education, etc. This is also all the more difficult to make sense out of because one of the images of the pastor in recent years has been that of an "administrator," or a "pastoral director."

Then there's the matter of those non-traditional functions that we could put under the heading of the "therapeutic." That's a little harder to explain since it seems to depart the most from the traditional functions of pastors. But is it really such a departure? Therapy is really just a different modern word for healing. Pastors have traditionally been known as "physicians of the soul," as healers. Maybe the main difference is, though, that we've learned from a new source, primarily the psychological and social sciences of the modern day. After all, isn't this the real meaning of "tradition" down through history? That we have taken the best of insight into man from the age in which the church has existed and used it for the benefit of man? I think it is. We're in danger of trying to make yesterday's truth fit today's need. Today's need calls for competent therapists, and that's what we are—as *true* traditionalists!

Another thing which ought to be looked at is the way in which hospitals don't let chaplains be pastors to the hospital itself. There aren't many staff members who feel that the chaplains can do anything for *them*. No sir, it's only the patients who need the chaplain; we don't have human needs, well certainly not *religious* needs.

How do you point out the fact that the work of the local parish pastor, as he works with his church boards, helps with the financial planning for the church, plans for the future expansion of his church, doesn't have much of a parallel in hospital chaplaincy? Oh sure, you get put on a few committees—don't forget to mention the library committee—but in most ways you're quite a ways down on the totem pole. Admit it—you envy your colleagues in the parish ministry a bit at this point. But it really is too bad the hospital pastor isn't allowed to make the contribution here he could make.

It's a struggle for power.

You get involved in professional jealousies.

What could a "pastor" know about a hospital?

(Don't answer that phone, ignore it, you're beginning to get a few ideas now.)

What *is* really needed in hospital chaplaincy? I guess to get right down to the primary thing, we need a lot more clinical collaboration.

Everybody talks about collaboration but it's mostly talk. Big-name physicians and clergymen talk on "high levels" like it was a reality, but down here on the grassroots level you know it's mostly talk. Most psychiatrists and chaplains still work in isolation. (But you'd better set this in perspective—most *all* professions seem to be much too isolated from one another.)

You can't tell a professional how he *ought* to act.

What he *ought* to do.

How he *ought* to treat you.

You have to earn his respect, earn your way onto his team. That's the way it's done. You've got to earn his respect, then he *may* accept you.

There's so much professional prejudice around you every day. Today you read more and more about the "human values," the "rights" of patients. The public isn't going to put up forever with having their needs set aside while professional groups squabble. (You're getting away from the subject.)

Some psychiatrists think only psychiatrists know anything about the human mind. All physicians practice some form of psychiatry. Few, if any, ministers could be part of any therapeutic program.

That's what they *think*. You're going to *teach them* differently? Good luck. You've got your work cut out for you.

Paternalism in any form tends to be abhorrent to you when it keeps human needs from being met.

Enough of that.

Let's assume the chaplain's really "on the team." How could he work with the psychiatrist? We certainly have to start with the psychiatrist because he has the legal responsibility. He certainly ought to be utilized as a diagnostic consultant. The chaplain has had a lot of experience and training in relation to religion, he's had clinical and academic training in the psychological and social sciences, he certainly has a perspective that will be helpful. We hear a lot of talk today about values in therapy. That's kind of what religion's all about, isn't it?

You could point out how Stein and Thomas reported a short while ago in one of the hospital journals on the importance of the chaplain as a member of the diagnostic team. They found it was especially difficult for the psychiatrist when the patient was of a different religious background than the psychiatrist. This is where the chaplain has a contribution to make.

If you had time you might point out the difficulty you had in even getting invited to the diagnostic staff meeting. How getting to be present at a staff meeting doesn't make you part of it, even then. How it's an uphill struggle, and even now after several years you're still working on it.

It's getting a little off the subject but you wonder about the training of the mental health professions, especially the psychiatrists. You seem to remember reading somewhere that a physician by the name of Kepler has suggested all of medical education needs to take a new look at the place of human values in the educational process—that also means a look at religion. Not a passing glance, but the need to take it seriously and study it as one would study other things in the curriculum. Little wonder mental health professionals don't understand the chaplain or his work. Where would they learn this? They just don't have the perspective. So you have to try to fill this gap in their education.

But you've educated so many. They keep coming and going. You start again and again. This is strictly a second-best way of doing it.

There's going to be real collaboration between psychiatrist and chaplain? Some one's going to have to give some administrative attention to that. Start keeping you informed. Change some of their traditional ways of thinking. How come most hospitals have forms for just about every profession to be used in patient records, but no form for chaplains? Of course, no one thought of it! Ten years from now when they change the forms again they'll see what can be done to correct it. (Careful, Artie, you said you'd try to keep your sense of humor.)

You know one thing, though, hospital administrators need a little updating here. What do *they* expect of a chaplain? You also remember that in another piece of research Golden showed (by the most acceptable research methods!) that chaplains tended to be doing what they thought was expected of them. And if the administration of the hospital expects little or nothing of them—.

A similar kind of case could be made for the use of the chaplain as a consultant in psychotherapy, as it was in relation to diagnosis. If we recognize the importance of values in psychotherapy there is no way we can bypass the chaplain. The chaplain then becomes a full team member. He has his area of expertise to contribute to the therapeutic program of the patient just as does the psychologist, the social worker, the occupational therapist, the physician—all the professions that are there to serve the person. He's going to have to work, though, to be that much a part of the team. He may even have to *fight* for it.

Why are religious people always expected to be *meek*? What's wrong with fighting for the opportunity to meet the religious needs of persons? You're tempted to give up sometimes, to retreat, but you try not to "yield to temptation."

Now, let's carry this whole thing one step further, let's suggest that the chaplain should also find his identity by being in his own right a "religious therapist." There'll be a lot of objection to that way of putting it, but that's O.K. In the setting of the mental hospital that's the way it has to be said. On the "outside" you might use the euphemistic term "pastoral counselor," but here you're a "religious therapist."

That is to say as a clergyman you have your own values and religious tradition of which you are a part, and which has produced you. You have your own goals in working with persons, your own ways of responding to human need. You have the resources of religion that include everything from religious words to sacraments. And you use this in being a true pastor to people. As you work with patients you may want to call upon the social worker, or the psychiatrist, or some other staff member to be *your* consultant, to help you accomplish *your* goals with the patients.

Many of the mental health professionals have a lot of trouble with this one. They are unaware that the very term "mental health professional" tags them and restricts their understanding of persons. A psychiatrist by the name of Howland pointed this out to you. "Mental health professionals" are part of a movement that has a conception of mental health that subsumes and subordinates religion and religious concerns. Unless they can understand this, unless they admit this is true they will never understand why the chaplain is *really* there, much less have any idea of what he could possibly do as a "religious therapist."

O.K. that could be kind of a beginning, but there seems to be something missing. What *is* a chaplain anyway?

Religious therapist.

Jester?

I have always been convinced of the importance of history. In our personal lives it is to a large extent our ability to understand our past history that makes it possible for us to come to full awareness of who we are in the present. I think the same thing is true of professions, so let's take a look at the chaplaincy from this perspective. (Sounds like we are getting a little serious here. But that's O.K. too.)

Chaplaincies have been around a long time, and one thing we note is that they have had different structures, intents, underlying theologies, even different financial backing. We can assume that this is all right because different situations, different historical periods, have called for differences in ministry. Perhaps, however, it is fairly accurate to make the generalization that most chaplaincies, up to World War I, were what might be best described as "parochial and parenthetical." One good illustration of this was the practice of the Roman Catholic Church in assigning retired priests to an institution with their duty being that of "chaplain"— having the duty solely to conduct a sacramental ministry. I hope that it is clear that by current standards for chaplains such ministries would be considered as definitely substandard.

Plummer makes an interesting observation at this point. He says that the use of clergy as chaplains in this way, e.g., only for a sacramental ministry, reflects the influences of Platonism on theology, especially as further delineated by Descartes, which resulted in the definition of the chaplain's area of concern as being "the almost biological entity of the soul." So here we see the adherence to a sacred/secular dichotomy which increasingly seems to find diminished acceptance in modern theology. Many today who tend to stereotype the chaplain's work, seeing him as only concerned with such things as prayers and sacraments, whether they know it or not, form their opinions of his work on a largely outmoded theological viewpoint—one which is no longer the underlying motivation for chaplaincy work. Nor for ministry in general. Outstanding examples of the new stance for clergy may be seen in the Roman Catholic Father Daniel Berrigan, and the Protestant Dr. Martin Luther King, Jr.

So there is an entirely new concept of chaplaincy today which began about fifty years ago. One major source of its beginning was a group of avant-garde clergy who began what we know as clinical pastoral education. Here the medical model was used in regard to the "clinical" aspect of the clergyman's preparation for his ministry. This group also generally championed Freudian theory and relied heavily on the behavioral sciences. Thus there developed a clergyman with a new orientation, usually entering some type of chaplaincy work, who was prepared to be a full treatment-team member. As we have seen however, such clergymen have not always been allowed to function as full team members, and the fact that they are prepared to do so does not automatically negate the old sacred/secular dichotomy in the minds of other professionals.

Now, assuming the readiness of the chaplain to serve, how does the chaplain become related to an institution? How is the context of his ministry to be seen?

Many chaplains have come from what is called the "free-church tradition." From this tradition the chaplain sees *the hospital as church*, and assumes that his ministry would be basically the same as if he were serving a church anywhere else. He carries on his work, remains in fellowship with other churches and clergy. Here, as we can see, the concept of "church" is that it is the local congregation, in this case the hospital, which associates itself for fellowship and service with other churches.

The chaplain's ministry has been seen from another point of view as essentially *a ministry of the church to institutions.* In this point of view the ministry belongs to the church (i.e., the clergyman's denomination. council of churches, etc.). His work is solely that of a pastor (usually) representing his church's ministry *to* the institution. In a large measure this view, in my personal opinion, perpetuates the old sacred/secular dichotomy.

Quite in contrast to these views is the view of the chaplain as *solely a treatment-team member.* Here nearly all relationship to church or denomination is lacking, although the chaplain does possess ordination. Ordination is, however, seen as merely a formality to permit functioning as "a mental health professional." Other than the fact that this chaplain conducts a religious service on Sunday there is little to distinguish him from any other member of the health team. Such a stance for a chaplain is not hard to understand, since so many chaplains today are the employees of civil rather than religious institutions. The chaplain may well see himself as in a similar position to physicians or psychologists, for example, who hold their professional standing in their appropriate "association," and work in an institution on the basis of the rights and privileges which accrue to persons with that professional standing.

(My, but we are getting serious, aren't we? Better get a cup of coffee before . . . we put . . . ourself to sleep . . .)

Now it would seem to me that the ideal would be for the chaplain to be related to his institution—and here I'm thinking primarily of the chaplain in the mental hospital—in a way that would fall sort of in between the previous positions mentioned. It is possible to conceive of the chaplain as *both clergyman and full member of the health team.* After all, isn't that the situation with all other professionals on the team? It's certainly something to think about.

It has been my feeling for some time that among all professionals who come to work in a hospital the chaplain has the most difficulty because of the common stereotype which sees him as a nonmedical professional. I think this is especially hard to accept since many chaplains think of themselves as "physicians of the soul."

I have often wondered how well accepted a physician would be on the staff of a church. Would he ever be accepted as a member of the religious team, or would he always really be seen as a nonreligious professional?

So, I think there have been great strides made toward an integrated view of chaplaincy, but as yet they are incomplete.

But basic to all of these concerns, issues, and problems about chaplaincy, is the question of whether or not the chaplain has anything to contribute to health care. Behind this lies still another issue—what is the relation of religion to health?

There are some who think that in health care we have passed beyond the old radical/materialistic stance that so thoroughly characterized the early years of this century. (While to some it may be obvious, this old view was simply another way of stating the old sacred/secular theology.) If this is true, and it is patently obvious to me that both science and medicine *have indeed* moved beyond this old materialistic view, and if we are now ready to affirm the reality of the non-material, the spiritual, then we stand at a point where the door has opened to the contribution of religion, primarily through its ordained "professional" in the hospital.

If we were to assume the relevance of religion to healing and the presence of competently trained clergy in a hospital, what would be their contribution? I'd like to adapt some remarks made by Stuart A. Plummer and his colleagues and suggest that a chaplain would function:

1. As a restorer of health (holiness) to persons.

2. As a specialist in the spiritual aspect of patient care.

3. As a source of compassion dedicated toward the full recognition of the uniquely "human" aspect of patient need.

4. As a person competent to assist in articulating and examining the value questions inherent in that experience and setting.

5. As "one who stands with others" (patient, families and staff) in the face of situations which are manifestly unmanageable and confront all persons with their ultimate limits and helplessness.

6. As a prophetic and reconciling agent where individual and corporate value systems are in conflict and may dehumanize persons.

7. As a "bridge" and "critic" between institution, church and community.

8. As a "facilitator" and enabler of ministry (by institution and church).

9. As a potential "advocate" for the patient/inmate/client.

10. As an explicit "spokesman" for the ministry of the institution within which he serves.

Appendix

Letters to family members about the strange world of mental illness

I To Mr. & Mrs. Straighte concerning their daughter Cindy

"Why did this have to happen to us?"
"We just can't get away."
"What kind of hospital are you running?"
"What did we do wrong?"
The night is darkest just before the dawn.
Some day society will understand.

"Why did this have to happen to us?"

Dear Mr. & Mrs. Straighte,

Your letter was most welcome. The question you posed at the end of your letter is not an easy one to respond to. You ask: "Why did this have to happen to us?" I know that this question must be giving you considerable anguish. I wish that you were here so that we could sit down together and wrestle with that question, it is so difficult to try to respond by means of a letter.

Several other questions you asked are a lot easier for me to respond to. You may be interested in knowing that your daughter's situation was carefully discussed yesterday at a staff meeting. I am pleased to be able to say that the staff feels that your daughter is doing well, she is much better than when she came here three weeks ago; however, I must also say that the staff did not feel that she is ready to leave and return to her husband and children at this time.

Your question about the prognosis and when she will be able to leave, I will respond to as best I can. This morning I spoke to her psychiatrist. He says that he hopes you will find it possible to visit here soon, at which time he will be happy to answer any questions you may have. You see, he is hesitant, as I am, of putting labels on people. We prefer to see persons rather than labels. While he did say that your daughter was considered very ill when she arrived, he spoke optimistically about expected return to life outside the hospital. Of course, we cannot set any arbitrary time as to when she will be released. The important thing is that she becomes well. When that time comes, I can assure you that we will help her in every way to prepare to resume her life outside the hospital.

If you can find it possible to visit here soon, perhaps we can sit down together and wrestle with your question, "Why did it have to happen to us?"

Sincerely,
A.K.

"We just can't get away."

Dear Mr. & Mrs. Straighte,

Yes, I certainly do know how difficult it is to get away from important matters. Cindy will be disappointed when I tell her that you probably won't be able to come to visit her at this time. I guess the fact that both of you are professional people really requires that you devote considerable time to your work, and the trip from Philadelphia certainly would be long and tiring. I must say I am disappointed also because I was looking forward to meeting you in person and discussing with you the question you posed in your first letter.

Meanwhile I understand that there is a good possibility that Cindy may be spending a weekend at home soon with her husband and children. Since you cannot come to visit her at this time, I hope you will find it possible to write to her regularly as she very much needs such expression of your love.

Sincerely,
A.K.

"What kind of hospital are you running?"

Dear Mr. & Mrs. Straighte,

Let me say that I was just as much shocked as you at what transpired last weekend. I hope you will accept my assurance that we felt quite confident that there would be no problem when Cindy visited at home. Most important of all, we can be thankful that the children were not harmed and that Cindy herself escaped physical injury.

As you requested, I spoke to the clinical director and he has asked me to pass along what we know. The decision to let Cindy go home for the weekend was made by the staff of Cindy's unit. The staff felt that the home visit and the chance to be with the children would be the best possible therapy for her.

As we had arranged, John came Saturday morning and took Cindy home. He was somewhat late as he had trouble with the old car he was driving. Cindy took with her enough medication for the two days she was to be gone. She was to be back Sunday night at 6:00 P.M. We cannot be sure of all that happened during the day on Saturday. When John called the hospital he seemed pretty upset. However, I guess they had a quarrel during the day and John decided it would be better if he got out of the house for a while until things cooled down. When he returned he found his car gone and Cindy and the children too. He says he made a number of phone calls, and when she didn't return he called the police and reported her missing. The rest of the story you have is essentially correct. Cindy ran off the road with the car and did extensive damage to it. Maybe her guardian angel was watching over her, but it certainly does seem a miracle that neither she nor the children were hurt.

When I saw Cindy on the ward Sunday morning just before the chapel service, she was still naturally quite upset. She felt she had tried to harm the children and couldn't understand why. It was also difficult for her to accept the fact that the children have been placed, temporarily, in someone else's home. However, I have assured her, and I would like to assure you, that these homes are very carefully selected by the Family Service Agency and that the children will be well taken care of.

I certainly can understand your feelings toward the hospital, and I do not want to have us sidestep our responsibilities in any way. However, there is always an element of risk when we let a person assume greater responsibility—and I am sure that we even make errors in judgment at times. In any case, let's be thankful that no one was physically injured and that the children are being well taken care of.

You may also be interested in knowing that Cindy has expressed interest in psychodrama and will be attending her first session later this week. Sometimes this form of therapy is able to be of considerable help to the patients.

I remain confident that as we all pull together we will see progress for Cindy. Meanwhile, please write to Cindy; your letters are important to her.

Sincerely,
A.K.

"What did we do wrong?"

Dear Mrs. Straighte,

When you phoned this morning, you certainly surprised me—it was a good surprise, however, and now I feel I know you better. This helps me when I talk with Cindy. As Cindy wrote to you, we have talked together a number of times. I can understand how you feel so deeply hurt by what she has written to you. None of us finds it easy to look honestly at ourselves as parents.

For me the question you posed, "What did we do wrong?" is linked with the question you raised in your first letter. I wish there was some easy way of finding answers to such questions. These questions nag away at us and raise up all sorts of doubts and other questions. They open old sores and shake the very foundations of our lives.

Basically, we are not interested in determining "who was right and who was wrong." Such considerations may have a place in a court of law, but they are quite out of place in relation to mental healing. There is little doubt, as I am sure you can attest from your own experience as a teacher, that parents do not always act wisely. In fact, I gather that at the present time you may even wonder if you did anything right. I hope you will let such deep searching serve as a springboard toward establishing a new relationship with your daughter.

Whatever has been your relationship to Cindy in the past cannot be changed now, but you certainly can take a long honest look at your relationship as it now exists. I see Cindy's criticism of you as a way of letting out things that have been bottled up inside her for many, many years. Her anger and hurt are now rushing out in torrents, and need to come out. But if you can accept her now, anger and all, and still love her, then I am sure that you will provide one of the most necessary ingredients for her healing.

I see you as a searching, growing person. Perhaps, in a way, Cindy's healing may also be a healing for you.

Sincerely,
A.K.

The night is darkest just before the dawn.

Dear Mr. & Mrs. Straighte,

This morning I sat in on the unit staff meeting where Cindy's progress was discussed in some detail. I am happy to say that there is unanimous agreement as to the fact that she is making exceptional progress. I think by now you must have noticed a change in the tone of her letters. As she has said to me in our talks, the fact that you still wrote to her and stuck by her even in spite of all the things she has written to you over the past number of weeks—this has helped her to believe you must really love her. She still has her doubts, but they are doubts that she feels she can now speak about in a more reasonable way.

Apparently Cindy has also been helped much by her participation in psychodrama. The psychologist tells me that when she first attended the meetings she would hardly say a word, but in the last several sessions she has spoken more freely, and on one occasion she volunteered to take the part of a mother in a family scene. She first played the role of "bad-mother"—it was a marvelous performance. When it was suggested she take the role of "good-mother" she found it very difficult. When the "children" misbehaved she found it most difficult to still be loving and accepting of them. The psychologist feels that she has made a good beginning toward understanding her own difficulty in giving love—and in receiving it too. She will be continuing in psychodrama. We are hopeful that she will soon be able to recreate for us the scene in which the car ran off the road.

At this time the staff feels she is near the point where she can try another visit home—with her husband, but not the children. Perhaps we are a little overly cautious at this point, but we want to be sure it is a good experience for her.

I hope you will write again soon. How are things going with you and your struggle to make sense out of Cindy's hospitalization?

Sincerely,
A.K.

Some day society will understand.

Dear Mrs. Straighte,

Yes, things are certainly going well. How thrilled Cindy was when she heard the children had returned home with John. Then, to have the staff decision to release her after one more weekend visit with the children and John—well, she can hardly wait.

The thing that I note in particular is the new positive attitude she has. You remember how she used to continually berate herself and in particular how she dwelt on that episode of the car accident. Now she feels that she has a good beginning understanding of herself and she has learned to have faith in herself—much of which she attributes to the fact that you accepted her, anger and all, and continued steadfast in your love.

Since you have raised the subject, yes, I had wondered why you had never come to visit Cindy. Your willingness to look more honestly at your reasons for not doing so say to me that this experience has become for you a growing experience, too. As you say, here you are, a well-educated professional person, yet you find that you share, unconsciously, in the general attitude of society toward mental illness. Perhaps some day society will understand. Certainly your example of looking honestly at your reactions, feelings, and your willingness to apply a little reason to your attitudes sets an example for those around you. But most important of all, having thrown aside the confining chains of the stigma of mental illness, you are in a better position to be the kind of mother that Cindy still needs very much.

You will need to have faith and patience in regard to your husband, too. It may take him a little longer to achieve the same understanding of mental illness which you have achieved. In his work he has been further removed from people than you. It takes time to throw off the old ingrained stereotypes and prejudices. Certainly I trust that he will be able to do this and that he will find this to have been a growing and enriching experience just as you have.

I guess I was about as excited as Cindy to learn that, since Cindy's leaving the hospital coincides with your spring vacation, you will be spending a few days with her when she first returns home to help her with the house and children. If your schedule permits, please stop by the hospital and say "hello."

Sincerely,
A.K.

"He's really sorry."
"Who's to blame?"
Facing up to reality.
Sometimes a son just needs his father.
The first step out.

"He's really sorry."

Dear Mr. Torridson,

Mike has asked me if I would be willing to write to you and say that he's really sorry for all that happened. I am just beginning to get acquainted with Mike and so I am still struggling to understand his present situation.

Obviously, Mike wants to set things straight between the two of you. If there is any way I can be of help, please let me know.

Sincerely,
A.K.

"Who's to blame?"

Dear Mr. Torridson,

It must indeed be a difficult experience for you to accept the fact that Mike is a patient here at the hospital. Your question "Who's to blame?" is a natural one and indicates that you are seeking answers which will help to make sense out of the present situation.

Just in case the word has not reached you, let me say that I learned this morning that Mike is being transferred to a special ward here for drug abusers. This was not an arbitrary decision. Mike was interviewed by the staff of that ward, along with three other patients with drug problems, for one vacancy that had just occurred on the ward. The reason that Mike was chosen was that he seemed to have the greatest desire to really get hold of himself and get things straightened out. This is an encouraging indication that Mike should do very well in the treatment program.

I know that parents of young people with drug problems naturally tend to blame themselves. They say: "If only I had been a little stricter," or "Why didn't I spend more time with the kid." It's good to ask serious questions, but don't be too hard on yourself, that doesn't really help much. I'm sure that, as you say, the fact that Mrs. Torridson died when Mike was so young has made it extra difficult for you. Should you have married again? I don't think anyone can answer that question, except perhaps you. In the past few years I have come to know a number of young people with drug problems. I find it impossible to point to any one thing that "makes them that way." It is an exceedingly complex problem.

But it is important that you come to understand your son better and have a clearer understanding of your relation with him. In fact, his progress here is linked to that. Notice that in stating it this way I am avoiding the placing of "blame" on anyone. I know that from your point of view it may seem like we are trying to determine who is to blame. First you had the visit from the police. Then, after Mike was hospitalized you received a long questionnaire from the hospital asking about family background and all sorts of personal things. Then you were asked to come in and answer more questions. It all seemed so impersonal to you. It was almost like we were trying to get enough facts so we could decide on some kind of court sentence. But let me assure you that we are not a court or a jail, we are a hospital. Our only purpose is to help Mike and you at a most difficult time for both of you.

One way that we can help the most is if we have a chance to meet you personally. Since Mike is allowed to have visitors this coming week, I hope you will stop by and say hello to me on your way to see Mike.

Sincerely,
A.K.

Facing up to reality.

Dear Mr. Torridson,

Since I am aware that your business trips will keep you from seeing Mike for a few weeks, I thought I would write to you to bring you up to date in regard to Mike. I think some real changes are taking place.

Perhaps I could best sum up what I see happening by saying

that Mike is beginning to face up to reality. But at the same time I have to say that the reality that Mike is beginning to face up to is a little different than what some of us "older" folks see.

Mike not only shares the long hair and whiskers of so many young people today, he shares many of their values as well. As you know, when Mike first came here he had very little to say. When I first saw him sitting silently in the corner of the ward, I thought he looked like a meditating Buddha; I wondered if he ever would speak. Believe me, he's speaking now! When you get back he's prepared to have a lot of questions thrown at you. Here are a few samples: My old man uses alcohol all the time, so what's wrong with popping a few pills? The church always taught me to love my fellow man so now I have to face the draft and take my turn killing people. Does that make any sense? If the whole purpose of religion is to transcend the self, what's wrong with using drugs to do it?

Well, those are just a few sample questions, so brace yourself! I take these questions quite seriously. One thing I note is the religious tone to many of the questions that Mike poses. I guess he's trying to make some sense out of what he learned through all those years you so faithfully sent him to Sunday School. And he's having a hard time of it. Frankly, these questions shake me. I think they require some honest answers and some honest searching on our part.

Take that first question. I readily admit that I enjoy a relaxing drink occasionally in the evening and I find that a cocktail at a party helps to make the occasion a little more fun. So how do I say to a young person "you can't smoke your pot"? Well, that's the bind we're in, isn't it? So you see I struggle with these questions too. It's a mark of our age, we struggle with some very important questions.

Mike comes across to me as a fellow who is basically very kind and gentle by nature. When he talks about peace and love a certain glow seems to permeate him. I think this is a side of Mike we all ought to get in touch with. I see it as an indication of a certain kind of strength that will surely hasten Mike's healing.

At the same time, I don't want to minimize the seriousness of Mike's situation. Of course, the final decision of the court will depend quite a bit on our recommendation. Mike is afraid you will try to influence the judge, whom he says you know. When I talked to him this afternoon he said: "Please tell Dad this is my thing, let me do it."

But I feel very optimistic about Mike's situation. I think being here is good for him. Better to come here now and face up to reality, than to go any further down the road he was traveling.

May I suggest you drop just a brief note to Mike while you are away. I think it would be important to him.

Sincerely,
A.K.

Sometimes a son just needs his father.

Dear Mr. Torridson,

Believe me, I envy your getting a suntan this time of year. The weather here has been just plain cold. Isn't there some way we can swap places?

I guess I just have to be honest and say I hope you won't prolong your business trip. There are times when a son just plain needs his father.

The main reason I say this is that the staff here feels that Mike is ready for a weekend home visit. There is no one else whom we consider appropriate for Mike to go out with at this time. As you realize, I am sure, the main factor that led to Mike's hospitalization was a poor choice of friends. I don't mean it is all really that simple, but associating with the right kind of people is important, and it is especially important right now for Mike as he is struggling to find himself and sorting out the values by which to order his life. My feeling is that right now he needs you. I hope you can be here.

I hope you'll forgive me if I anticipate a question on your part. I can hear you ask, "But what can I do for him now that couldn't wait for a couple of weeks?" So let me reply to that question by saying that maybe it's not so much a question of "doing" anything as it is a matter of "being" something. Mike needs a father. He needs an anchor point. No ship can ride out a storm in a harbor without a good strong anchor. (As an old Navy man you don't need me to tell you about that.) Frankly John, I think it's hard for Mike to feel he has any anchor when you bounce around so much with your business commitments. If you can't slow down your pace a bit perhaps you could find another anchor point for Mike. Isn't there anyone who could be a "substitute father" in your family? At least, something will have to be done to provide Mike with a little more of a stable living situation. We are ready to work with you toward that end.

Mike appreciated your letters a lot. Sometimes I think he tries not to let it show, but I think that basically he really likes you.

> Sincerely,
> A.K.

The first step out.

Dear Mr. Torridson,

I just don't know what to say to you except "congratulations" on being a true father to Mike last weekend. The staff feels Mike has truly taken the first step out. I guess I don't have to tell you—but I will anyway—how great he looked when he came back. The remark that really seemed to wrap it all up was when he said to me, "Hey, man, that dad of mine actually took time to rap with me."

Your desire to take Mike out of here as soon as possible is certainly understandable. However, it is at this point that I think it is necessary for you to put some trust in us. Far too many times I have seen relatives push for release of a patient. And sometimes, against their better judgment, the staff acquiesces and lets the patient go sooner than would ordinarily be the case. All too often we have come to regret letting ourselves be coerced, for sometimes even a few days makes the difference between whether or not a patient will have to return to the hospital. So again I say, trust us in our judgment of what is best for Mike.

Of course, Mike's final disposition will depend on the court. We feel reasonably confident, however, that the court will accept our recommendation. It is my understanding, having been present at several staff meetings where Mike's progress was discussed, that if he continues with the steady progress he has evidenced so far, we will probably recommend to the court that he be released to your custody. If this is done, one of the key questions that is sure to be asked is, "What is the situation at home?" I know this poses some serious issues for you, especially in regard to business trips, so the answer will not be easy. If I can be of help to you in this regard, please remember I am always available to you.

Well, I told Mike I'd see him today and we'd "rap" a bit.

Sincerely,
A.K.

About the Author

Ward A. Knights, Jr., a native of Bennington, Vermont, is Supervisor of Clinical Pastoral Education, St. Joseph's Hospital, Saint Paul, Minnesota. He is a graduate of John Brown University, Andover Newton Theological School (M.Div. & S.T.M.) and Vanderbilt University (D.Div.).

A minister of the United Church of Christ, Dr. Knights has served as chaplain at the Apple Creek State Hospital, Apple Creek, Ohio; the Cleveland Psychiatric Institute; and the New Hampshire Hospital, Concord, New Hampshire. He has also been minister of churches in Goshen and Plainfield, Massachusetts; First Congregational Church, Rochester, Massachusetts; Mystic Congregational Church, Medford, Massachusetts; and from 1945 to 1947 was with the 24th Division Artillery, U.S. Army. Dr. Knights is a Certified Supervisor of the Association for Clinical Pastoral Education and is the author of numerous journal articles, and the essay "The Role of the Chaplain in the Mental Hospital" in *Clinical Psychiatry and Religion*, ed. E. Mansell Pattison, 1969.